HONORABLE DESIGN

THE ART AND ORDER OF
GENERATIONAL TRANSITION

[THE SEIRA GROUP]

JERRY W DAVID, D.MIN. AND STEVE STELLS, D.MIN.

WITH MIKE SERVELLO

ISBN: 978-1-949856-06-4 (paperback), 978-1-949856-07-1 (epub)

Brookstone Publishing Group
P.O. Box 211, Evington, VA 24550
BrookstoneCreativeGroup.com

Ordering Information:
Special discounts are available on quantity purchases by corporations, associations, and others. For details, contact
Brookstone Publishing Group at the address above.

tioning. Leadership transitioning, like death, is inevitable and the authors have smoothly given a simple course of action to avoid chaos for organizations who desire to grow and remain healthy after leadership exits. If you are a leader and truly believe you should impart before you depart, you must read this book!"

—Frederick M Wyatt III
Pastor Fred Wyatt Speaking Spirit Ministries

"Passing the baton to the next generation is one of the most important lessons that Christ taught His disciples.

This volume provides the reader with biblical principles for skillfully passing the baton to the next generation. Christ for the Nations Ministry and Bible Institute is celebrating its 70th anniversary. As CEO and President, I am presently in the process of passing the baton to my three children, which was first handed to me by my parents, thirty-three years ago. This volume provides the essentials for generational succession and is truly a masterpiece. It has assisted me remarkably."

—Dr. Dennis Lindsay
CEO and President Christ for the Nations Ministry and Bible Institute

"A typical millennial pastor responded to his aging ministry father, "I need your shoulders and you need my eyes." In this powerful book, both parties are taught to honor. I have seen nothing better on this important, critical subject for the worldwide church than this book. Seven years after releasing Bethany Church to the next generation, our church is continually breaking attendance records and planting more campuses. If you are wavering in this decision, here is the book to give you complete confidence!"

—Larry Stockstill
Pastor and Church Planter

"This book marks out the problem principles of generational transfer and the practicalities of what every leader must know to make it happen."

—Bishop Wellington Boone
Chief Prelate, Fellowship of International Churches

"I am always fascinated to see how one generation hands off the succession of their church to another generation. The Bible talks about, "He's the God of Abraham, Isaac, and Jacob." I have seen some very unfortunate transitions and I've seen some very successful transitions. Without a doubt, Jerry David and Steve Stells have found great wisdom and are sharing some incredible truths of how to see to it that you build a legacy for the next generation and how to empower the next generation. I recommend this book to you as a great example of Godly succession and leadership."

—Pastor Steve Kelly
Senior Pastor of Wave Church

"*Honorable Design* is an excellent source of vital information presented by a team of highly qualified ministry consultants to assist pastors and ministry leaders in their midlife and beyond. This well-written guide contains biblically sound and practically-proven steps that leaders of churches and ministries can take to secure the future of their organizations and preserve their own legacies. Useful psychological principles and helpful business concepts are woven together in this book with a theologically balanced understanding of church and ministry to provide a comprehensive plan for leadership transition and succession. This plan can be adapted by organizations of all sizes. As a participant observer of several successful and some disastrous transitions within the Spirit-empowered movement, I highly recommend this book to churches and ministries across the world. Implementing the strategy proposed in this book is sure to reduce anxiety and pain in congregations and preserve the legacies of God's servants."

—Thomson K. Mathew, D.Min., Ed.D.
Professor of Pastoral Care and Former Dean
College of Theology and Ministry, Oral Roberts University

This is an incredible book with ten steps to assist all organizations to focus on transferring or building legacy and empowering the future generation. In my role as chief finance officer for a large non-profit organization, I normally think about two steps, viz. financial planning and core values. This book carefully crafted by David, Stells, and Servelo has made me realize the importance of the other 8 steps for a smooth and powerful transition of leadership in any organization. We have seen several churches and organizations going through confusion, pain, and distress when there is a sudden vacancy in the leadership. This is a great book for churches all over the world. I recommend this book for all Christian Fellowships, Churches and non- profit organizations to prepare and plan for a smooth transition.

—Dr. Durai Pandithurai
Chief Finance Officer, Salvation Army, TX

"Change is inevitable. Time marches on. Every church will, at some point, face transition in leadership. Successful transitions happen when preparation has been made to insure the success of the next generation of leadership. David, Stells and Servello have developed a model to assist pastors in the planning and execution of this plan. From their own experiences as well as working with countless pastors, their frank discussions of the issues that need to be faced and providing the framework for facing them, makes this book a must-read for all church leaders. Both timely and informative, their practical helps will lay a foundation for successful transition in all types of churches."

—Dr. Analee Dunn
Pastor-emeritus, Bethesda Christian Church

"This book is a must for every pastor and church who wants to do transition well to the next generation of leadership. The ten steps outlined in this book can save years of heartache and difficulty that most transitions face."

—Benny Perez
Lead Pastor ChurchLV.com

"The authors 90+ years of combined pastoral experience and sensitivity to church leadership in transition makes this a landmark book. It is a viable resource and workable templet for those who believe that the future belongs to the prepared. The practical guidelines, real life case studies, long overdue teachings and amazing quotes makes this book a timely must read."

—Dr. David Kiteley
Co-founder/Pastor Emeritus of Shiloh Church, Oakland Ca.

"Here is a book that every church leader should read—written and presented by three successful pastors that know what they are talking about. Believe me, they speak from experience. We all know that their basic premise is true: 'Sooner or later transition will happen in your church.' In fact, 60,000 churches in America will face transition this year! Pastors grow old, even die, new trends come and go, communities change and so does church leadership. There will always be transitions taking place, but church leaders simply are not trained to make pastoral transition the high-point or significant moment in that church's history.

The contents of this book will bring great wisdom to your time of change that is coming. No longer can we pastors say, 'Let's keep going and see what happens.' This attitude makes your transition 'a journey to nowhere!' Proverbs 29:18 says, *'Where there is no vision, the people perish.'* This great book is loaded with wonderful advice. Don't wait, these concepts are essential and should even now be working in the thinking of your church's leadership."

—Ernest Gentile
Pastor and Author

"The authors of this book are experienced, seasoned men of God who have served in His Kingdom nationally and internationally. Their thoughts are profound and appropriate to this season. Apostolic wisdom comes in many packages and this one is a particular blessing. If your church is passing through a transition of leadership here are the answers you need."

—Dr. Gary Munson, Ed.D., Th.D.
Chief Academic Officer, SUM Bible College & Theological Seminary

"This timely and inspiring book masterfully addresses the critical issue of pastoral leadership transition. When this issue is not handled wisely, a legacy built upon decades of successful and influential ministry can be unnecessarily sabotaged. Replete with practical guidelines and real- life examples, this book offers a strategy for leadership transition based upon proven principles and a culture of honor that will allow the legacy to survive and prosper."

—David W. Dorries, Ph.D.,
Teacher, Author and Director of Kairos Ministries International,
Lake Mary, Florida

"Succession is clearly central to the ways and mindset of a God who regularly referred to Himself as the God of Abraham, Isaac, and Jacob. Unfortunately, in today's church, failures in the area of succession planning is generally the rule, rather than the exception. A failure to plan in this critical area often results in unnecessary set-backs, loss of momentum and vision, and, in this consumer-driven age, the departure of clientele that in many cases has been many years in the making. The combined experiences and training of Jerry David, Steve Stells and Mike Servello fuels their ability to advance perspectives and protocols that are both scholarly and practical. Their fresh theological insights are tempered by life-long service as practitioners of pastoral leadership. This book is a must-read for all who serve in pastoral leadership and for those who train tomorrow's leaders."

—Dr. Pat Bopp
Instructor, in Practical Theology, Regent School of Divinity

"*Honorable Design* reveals the heart of these three former leaders to make pastors and churches successful in seasons of transition, something each has done brilliantly with their own pastorate, as well as helping multiple dozens of other pastors with their transition. In this book, they have married practical wisdom with a spirit of faith to inspire pastors and leaders to think about their future financially, and in life and ministry."

—Pastor Jude Fouquire
Senior Pastor, City Church, Ventura, CA

"Henry Ford said, 'Thinking is the hardest work there is, which is probably why so few engage in it.' David, Stells, and Servello shattered the notion set forth by Henry Ford. A must-read for denominational leaders to help guide those for whom this book was written."

—Dan Hicks
Sr. Associate Pastor The Church on the Way

"With four decades of pastoring in local churches as support staff or the Lead Pastor, I have experienced well-planned transitions and tornadic disasters leading to church splits or significant membership losses. I can confirm that what Jerry David and Steve Stells, along with Mike Servello, share in this essential book and the consulting wisdom they offer are priceless. Pastors, read it NOW!"

—Dr. Larry Keefauver
Former Senior Editor of *Ministries Today*,
Bestselling Author and International Teacher

"Transition mastery in an age of rapid, unprecedented, accelerated change is non-negotiable. The truth we need to embrace is that transition is a constant. All too often, the Church fails to discern the signs of its own times, let alone the signs of the culture, and know what to do about it. None of us will live forever, and the coming transition between generations is increasingly becoming evident in the passing of the torch of effectual leadership from the Baby Boomer generation to the Millennial generation. There are certain fundamental concepts that have to be "mastered" in transition from one generation to the next, if the vision of a local church is to be sustained over the long haul. Simply training pastors and leaders to 'preach the Text' is insufficient for sustainability.

"A careful look at Church History and we discover that the Spirit of God led those who have handed down the Tradition from generation to generation to use various methodologies and metrics by which to implement important initiatives as well as measure the results obtained by them. St. Paul refers to himself as a "wise master builder." (1 Corinthians 3:10)

If a pastor does not know the dynamics involved in being and becoming a wise-master builder, she or he will be at a great loss in terms of effectual, practical, sustainable ministry over the long haul, that passes on to the emerging generations the kind of gifts that they can grow on. *Honorable Design* is a thorough, well-written, precise practicum for all the things every pastor needs to know that they probably didn't get in their Bible College and Seminary training. The insights in this volume are a life-saving treasure-trove by three of the most effective transition-masters in the Body of Christ. Glean from their wisdom and apply it. It will serve you and the future you are serving well, as Jesus is calling us all from the future to the future, as the future is where you will be spending the rest of your life!"

—Dr. Mark Chironna
Church On The Living Edge
Mark Chironna Ministries, Longwood, Florida

DEDICATION

Today, the United States is experiencing the largest leadership exchange in its history. Pulpits are changing hands. Baby-boomers are retiring, and Millennials are replacing them at a furious rate.

We want to dedicate this book to all the leaders of our generation who heard the call, refused all other options, and chose to honorably dedicate their lives to extending the Kingdom of God through faithful service to His church and people.

Whether you served your congregation bi-vocationally, started a church in your living room, took over declining churches and saw them brought to life again, or did your part in the wider world—whatever the challenge, as leaders you persevered, remained faithful and are finishing your race strong.

We celebrate and honor you, and we cheer on those whom God is calling to take your place!

Acknowledgments

We wish to acknowledge our families and colleagues who encouraged us to write this book. We also thank the fellow leaders and teams who served with us throughout our pastorates, the congregants who received us as pastors, the teachers, mentors and professors who taught us, and most importantly, Jesus Christ who called and His Spirit who led, guided, instructed and empowered us to serve His people.

TABLE OF CONTENTS

AUTHORS

JERRY W. DAVID, D.Min., and his wife Susan founded and pastored Lincoln City Church in Lincoln, Nebraska for 25 years. This multi-ethnic, multi-generational church is now in its second generation of leaders and serves as an excellent example of continued and sustained leadership in the community and around the nation. Jerry currently serves as an Apostolic Leader with Ministers Fellowship International both in the USA as well as Singapore. With his forty plus years of pastoral ministry and leadership, he now finds himself strengthening other leaders and pastors throughout many nations and continents. He is noted for his inspirational preaching, teaching, and his transparent approach to today's practical leadership issues. His Doctorate, earned from Regent University, has prepared him specifically in the areas of Emotional Intelligence and Transformational coaching. Along with Steve and Mike, he is a partner with Seira Group, LLC., and Seira Financial Group, LLC., which specializes in working with local churches, nonprofits, and other organizations in transition and succession planning, at the leadership level.

STEVE STELLS, D.Min., and his wife Sharon founded and pastored The House of Prayer Church in Chesterfield, Virginia for 38 years. Today the church is a vibrant multi-campus church led by his oldest son.

Steve and Sharon live in Chesterfield and actively serve in the church they founded. Steve has served as an Apostolic Leader with Ministers Fellowship International (MFI) providing oversight to the Southeast Region of the United States for MFI. He also serves churches he helped plant along the east coast of the USA, and many that were partnered with in Europe, Asia, Africa and the Caribbean. With over forty plus years as a ministry leader, serving faithfully and with integrity, he is now called upon to advise, consult and coach ministry leaders. After earning his Doctorate from Oral Roberts University, Steve now partners with Jerry and Mike in Seira Group, LLC., assisting church leaders and their congregations, nonprofits, and other organizations in transition and succession planning.

CONTRIBUTING:

MIKE SERVELLO is the founding pastor of Redeemer Church, which was a church planted in 1981 and is now a large and growing church with four campuses in the upper New York area. Mike and his wife Barb have recently transitioned from the Senior Pastor role and have turned the church over to the next generation, led by their son. Mike is also the founder and President of Compassion Coalition, a ministry that annually provides over 4.5 million pounds of food and products to people in need throughout upstate New York and around the world. For many years, he has served on the Apostolic Leadership Team of Ministers Fellowship International as Vice-Chairman. Along with Jerry and Steve, Mike brings a vast wealth of experience and knowledge to the issues facing pastors and organizational leaders in succession planning and transition, and serves as a partner in Seira Group, LLC.

WHY YOU NEED THIS BOOK!

480,000! That's the number of churches that will experience a Pastoral leadership change in the next ten years, because of an aging baby boomer population. Chances are, you and your church are in that number. And this does not include the many leaders in charge of other organizations who will experience similar transitions to those of the church. Yet, many pastors, founders, CEO's, presidents, directors, board members, and committees, as well as the people they serve, are totally unprepared when it comes to succession planning and leadership transition. Organizational transitions affect human beings—it is always people who must embrace a new situation and carry out the corresponding change.

The planning and ultimate execution of a transition can be one of the most disconcerting and tumultuous seasons in the leader and follower's life. Without a clear understanding of what a shepherding shift does to the people in charge and those they serve, and in turn, the organization— the job of managing a leadership change can be difficult if directed poorly. The result can prove disastrous to the morale, vision, and stability of the organization. But we have discovered it is possible to avoid many painful conflicts when you are intentional to initiate transition in an honorable and orderly way.

There have been, over the course of several years, a great many books written about succession in the local church and non-profit environment. So many of these books are excellent reads, and every pastor/ leader contemplating transition in the place he/she leads, would benefit greatly by reading many of them.

However, the clear majority seem to concentrate on the individual leader's story (as opposed to a more general overview of the process and thinking needed for successful succession planning and transition). This isn't to say that greater understanding cannot be gained by reading or hearing about someone else's story—but ultimately, your story will be unique to you.

After an exhaustive investigation of the material available to pastors and leaders concerning this critical topic, we found a serious lack in addressing the general principles and standards that should be considered by every leader and organization. This book is designed to address those critical values. Although we can't touch on every possible scenario that each organization (being unique) would represent, we can offer a pathway of critical thinking to the reader. This book is designed to provoke and stimulate further understanding and a healthier approach to this timely topic.

Where are you and your organization on the leadership transition timeline? You may not realize how early you should begin to prepare and plan, in order to get the result you want. There's an art to the process.

Seira Group guides groups through the crucial steps of an honorable and orderly leadership transition—helping propagate necessary change with greater peace. We are available to consult with you before, during, and after the time of succession. We listen to you and learn about your needs, interview your team and key leaders, and then propose a consulting process that will help you and your group move forward and maintain momentum, until you achieve a satisfying outcome.

TRANSITION WILL HAPPEN! ARE YOU READY?

One's leadership style often comes to the surface as life happens, based on the individual's personality (determined by genetic make-up), formative experiences, education, or a combination of all three. How you as a leader will respond to a pending transition, or the effects of that transition, is determined primarily by your emotional health/maturity and wellness. A commitment to the art and order of an honorable succession design will prevent many problems and protect your organization.

Transitions happen in everyone's life—not just pastors of local congregations or leaders of large organizations. Historically, in countries like America where a succession takes place every four or eight years from one President to the next, we see a living example of the upheaval and emotional adjustment that such a transition has on a leader and the people he or she serves.

In their book, *7 Practices of Effective Ministry*, authors Andy Stanley, Reggie Joiner and Lane Jones relate the story of former President George H.W. Bush and the impact of his transition from the highest office in the land.

> "Shortly after President George H. W. Bush left office, our staff attended a conference where Bush was the keynote speaker. He described in detail his final flight on Air Force One after the inauguration of Bill Clinton. That day Bush woke up in the White House and went to bed in a rented house in Houston. He said that the next morning he woke early and started reaching around in the dark, trying to find the button that for years, had signaled the staff that he wanted a cup of coffee. He accidentally woke up Barbara, his wife, who figured out what he was trying to do. She said, 'George, you're just going to have to get up and go get it yourself. It's over!'" [1]

---

1 Andy Stanley, Lane Jones, Reggie Joiner. *The 7 Practices of Effective Ministry.* Sisters, OR: Multnomah Publishers, 2004. Pp 157-158

INTRODUCTION

The Elephant in the Room—
Sooner or Later Transition Will Happen

"No one wins when transitions don't go well."
—Ralph C. Wilkins

S uccession planning is a hot topic these days, as well it should be. We are experiencing a significant graying of senior leaders and ministers, and now many are considering their exit plans. Leadership transitions or exit planning should be a long-term process, not an "Oh my God, I'd better quickly put a plan together today, so I can step aside in a couple of days, weeks or months." Instead of peaceful, orderly, honorable, and successful transitions, most we've witnessed mirror exactly the scenario we just described. With disastrous results.

We chose the name Seira Group for our consulting business because of Seira's definition. It means *unbroken chain.* From our experience, you can predict the chain of events or life cycle of every church, non-profit organization, or company. For most, the links in the chain look roughly like this survival-mode method:

- "Midas" growth phase
- First stumble
- Success
- Second stumble

- Sustainability
- Decline

Each of these phases presents an opportunity to transition. But transition should not be entered into at many of these points—as the wrong timing will result in the extinction of your life's work. You can strengthen your ministry or entity, if you strategically create an honorable plan and place your chains in better order.

Sad to say, we see too many transitions taking place after the organization has begun to decline. You must understand, if a church or organization is not growing or expanding, it is declining. When a ministry or work is in decline, most decisions concerning transition are usually the wrong decisions. For instance, if the exiting leader is fatigued or discouraged, the decisions he or she makes regarding transition will most certainly be somewhat self-serving.

Successful transitions require scenario planning and strategic analysis. To maintain honor and order for everyone affected by the process, it's crucial to look at where the organization has been, where it is, and determine its goals for the future. Senior leaders preparing to move on may think the biggest transition for an influencer is retiring from full-time governance, but this is not necessarily so.

There are the rare occasions where unexpected circumstances force the expedited departure or transition of a leader. Moral failures, sudden death, and other extenuating situations can literally throw the entire organization into a state of uncertainty and confusion. Even so, much of this confusion could be eliminated. Having a good long-term succession plan in place and ready for implementation, prior to the blindsiding event, as opposed to making hurried, emotion-based decisions to meet a crisis need, can prevent unnecessary challenges or complete collapse.

When it comes to succession planning, we have found the perceptions of too many senior leaders, leadership teams, congregations, and other influencers to be nothing more than viewing a need for job placement, personnel change or meeting a hiring predicament. Nothing could be further from the truth, and nothing could insure organizational failure more than that type of approach.

Succession planning and the ultimate transition that accompanies it, is one of the most critical, emotional, fraught-with-danger moments in the history of any church or organization. To approach it with anything less than sobriety and a well-thought-out plan and commitment to eventual execution of that plan, courts disaster.

This is why today, from a ministry perspective, pastors can relate to more transition failures in churches than successes. We've all heard the horror stories, and sometimes have seen them played out in the news. Sadly, we're authoring this book from personal insight and experience, driven by our desire to help you prevent what has cost others dearly.

Our coaching and consulting ministry with pastors and their churches, as well as with other organizational heads, is a response to one primary issue every leader eventually faces in their history—the transitioning of senior influencers. Through the years, we have learned how to provide support, education, and equipping for those who have guided for decades, and then faced the frightening reality of leadership succession.

Most of our clients were founders. Each had a deep love for their people and felt a sense of great honor in shepherding. None had a moral failure, and all had served faithfully without becoming "famous." Their life and calling would not be different than most leaders in America today. They battled weariness and discouragement, as well as enjoyed the small victories that came from seeing lives changed in the people they cared for.

All sought personal growth relationships outside their organizations—evidencing a desire for leader-to-leader mentoring connections. It is the awareness of the need for (and maintenance of) safe relationships that seemed to keep, strengthen, and caution them as leaders. Those same supportive relationships kept them coming back to the work, week after week.

Relational associations propel pastors and leaders to cautiously seek other connections with like-minded influencers; and yet, when the topic of transition is broached, leaders often stop connecting. Why?

The reasons certainly cannot be traced to the behavior or teaching of Jesus—the ultimate example of a long-term, successful leader. He is the master of connection.

The reasons for silence among leaders in transition, instead of being grounded in spiritual principles, seem to be rooted more in fear and low self-confidence. The authors of *The Elephant in the Boardroom*[2] further suggest that leaders fear the following, if they talk about transition:

- Talking about transition might put the idea in someone's head and make it more likely to happen.
- Discussing future transition and succession will create a lame-duck situation in which effective productivity becomes impossible.
- Letting such transition conversations happen will have unintended consequences that we do not know how to manage.
- Having the resources to deal with transition planning and being successful at it, are lacking.
- Securing the support of peers and colleagues will be difficult, and the leader planning for the future will have to become a pioneer on the road of effective transition, even if it means "going it alone."

---

2 Weese, Carolyn and Russell J. Crabtree. *The Elephant in the Boardroom: Speaking the Unspoken about Pastoral Transitions.* San Francisco: Jossey-Bass, 2003 pp. 14-15.

In fact, becoming disconnected in any form can ultimately produce a fear, which paralyzes the individual from further discussion regarding transition.

Author Larry Crabb offers this powerful statement in his book, *Connections*:

> "Disconnection can be regarded as a state of being, a condition of existence where *the deepest part of who we are is vibrantly attached to no one, where we are profoundly unknown and therefore experience neither the thrill of being believed in nor the joy of loving or being loved (italics, his)*. Disconnected people may often be unaware of the empty recesses in their souls that long to be filled. They often mistake lesser longings for greater ones and settle for the satisfaction of popularity, influence, success, and intense but shallow relationships. Disconnected people are unaware of what God has placed within them that if poured into others could change lives. They feel either inadequate for questionable reasons or powerful for wrong reasons." [3]

No one likes to be disconnected or out of relationship with those we love. Jesus himself expressed that very emotion on His cross when he cried out, "My God, why have you forsaken me?" (Matthew 27:26)

Crabb encapsulates an understanding of the fears, anxiety, and identity issues that we believe leaders experience when the subject of transition presents itself. In speaking with scores of influencers who have transitioned out of the leadership role they once enjoyed, we have discovered the overwhelming majority will *still*—even *years* after their successor transitions—quickly identify themselves in a general conversation as "leader" or "founder" of such-and-such work.

---

3 Crabb, Larry. *Connecting*. Nashville, TN: Word Publishing, 1997 p. 37 5

We believe that the fear of disconnection, of no longer being wanted or needed, and of possible rejection or loss of identity, evidence a deficiency in emotional wellness. When coupled with insecurity and misplaced ego-related issues, we have found the chance for successful leadership transition is diminished—considerably.

With a combined total of over ninety years in leadership, we have watched too many hold on to their authority role well past their prime. Some attempt to transition their organization too late, others try to reclaim their position as fears increase, while a large percentage undermine their successor behind-the-scenes in such a way as to guarantee his or her failure. Others have transitioned out of their roles but never developed a meaningful life beyond the organizational helm. All of these produce unhealthy outcomes.

In *Honorable Design*, we will address this widespread problem within the leadership ranks by focusing on the emotional maturity and health of those in charge, exploring the needed mindsets and attitudes, as well as emotional and transitional strategies that will prepare the successor for what's coming. The future of your church or organization depends on the choices you make today. In other words, the purpose of the book, along with our work in connecting through coaching and consulting is to:

- Help and support the senior organizational leader, develop an awareness and understanding of (along with an emotionally healthy mindset and philosophy towards) your eventual transition from a senior authority role.
- Assist and support the designated new senior leader. Develop and form an orderly and emotionally healthy approach that will aid in setting forth principles and actions related to his/her eventual succession into the senior leadership role.

The goal is what could be described as **"an atmosphere of honor"** between the predecessor and successor. We have seen and experienced what many view as impossible, or at the very least, improbable. But this is how you ensure your organization's strong chain of influence continues.

Our leadership intervention as we connect with influencers, follows these important themes:

- Emotional awareness
- Successor relationships
- Transformational coaching

Success rates spike once **a paradigm of mutual honor** is established between the predecessor and successor. Securing commitments for future dialogue and transparency between the predecessor and successor, and in the context of that relationship, helps all involved to recognize and successfully deal with the unique emotional issues they face on a personal level in their leadership context—as well as in their transitioning public roles.

Join us on this journey of understanding successful leadership transition as we explore:

- the need for an atmosphere of honor
- the importance of emotional intelligence
- the purpose of clear, continual, and caring communication
- the primacy of values
- the priority of vision
- the significance of proper financial planning
- the practical implementation of a strategic plan with timelines, documentations, and execution
- the need for monitoring and evaluating the succession process
- the power of momentum
- the answers you need for how to move forward

"Typically people allow differences and mistakes to lower their respect and value for other people. But you know the pillar of honor is strong in a relationship when you can look at the other person and say, "You are really different from me. It makes me sad when I see you making that choice. But I love you. I value you, I believe in you, and I am here for you in this relationship."

— Danny Silk, *Keep Your Love On*

CHAPTER 1

HONORABLE DESIGN REQUIRES HONOR

"In a culture of honor, leaders lead with honor by courageously treating people according to the names God gives them and not according to the aliases they receive from people."

— Danny Silk, *Culture of Honor: Sustaining a Supernatural Environment*

America is going through the biggest pulpit exchange in its history, as are churches across the globe. But most transitions are not going well—due to lack of knowledge or planning. Businesses and non-profits are faring no better. If we do not protect our organizations from a negative turn, entire nations may pay the price. Successful succession is crucial to any country's health.

Mentoring smoothly from predecessor to successor creates an unbroken chain of leadership, saving the entity and its people. This makes way for the former to participate in a lasting legacy imprint, while the latter generates a fresh passion and fire in the people. If only Pastor John and Pastor Roger had known how to develop an honorable design, providing art and order for the generational transition they and their church so desperately needed.

A TALE OF PASSAGE BETWEEN TWO PASTORS

When he began to plan for his transition, Pastor John had led the church he founded in a large metropolitan area in the Southeast for almost forty years. The church had grown dramatically under his leadership, moving from a less than fifty-person congregation to a mega-church of about 3000 people. Training schools and Christian education outreaches were now included.

Pastor John's influence and that of the church was far reaching around the world by the time the planning process began. For his successor, he looked among the ranks of his "sons and daughters in the Lord," many who had been sent out, and successfully planted churches of their own. Pastor John eventually settled on Pastor Roger and invited him to take the reins of the senior leadership role. A timeline was established between the two men, as they developed a multi-year process that would culminate in transition.

The conversion timeline was broken up into three equal parts. Pastor Roger would first shadow Pastor John in all meetings and decisions; the second part would have both men working jointly on all decisions and vision related issues; with the last part of the succession plan making Pastor Roger the primary leader, while Pastor John took an observatory position. Both men later reported that, if they had to do it over again, they would not have orchestrated such a plan, or for so long of a period.

The side-effects were generally negative and almost fatal for the church. First, growing resentment developed between both men as Pastor Roger, a successful leader and now spiritual father in his own right, chaffed under the leadership of his mentor. Pastor John, sensing this, pushed even harder and did not make it easy for Pastor Roger to adjust to this new paradigm. It was evident that unaddressed insecurities and fears existed in both men. They were both masters in the Word of God and seasoned, as well as qualified, leaders of exceptional quality. But the pressures from the changes removed any evidence of honor in their relationship.

The last transitional worship service, passing leadership from one man to the other, left both men feeling emotionally drained and discouraged. Pastor John felt wounded and hurt that he had lost his place and influence. He had expected a certain level of honor and deference in keeping with his long history with the church and his work at bringing it to the point where it was. Pastor Roger left the service feeling insecure, like he would need to continually look over his shoulder. He felt resentful that, in his mind, Pastor John had treated him as less than a son. The congregation managed no better.

By the time the actual transition service took place, the congregation—because of the style and length of the transition, and by what they observed and assumed—had already been allowed to form their own opinions. Who was the *best*, or which man they would follow, were decisions already made. Disorder and disharmony ensued.

By the time the actual transition took place, the two leaders were divided against each other, the congregation felt disjointed and conflicted, and even far-reaching influencers expressed opinions and weighed in on the issue. Miraculously, the church did survive, but not without almost ten years of struggle and hard feelings only time would heal.

Pastor Roger was so injured in the process, that he rarely acknowledged Pastor John or the work he had accomplished. And although Pastor John occasionally attended services following the transition, he felt disconnected and without place or honor in the very house to which he gave his best years.

Theirs was supposed to be a model of the "right way" to pass the baton from one spiritual father to the next. A great host of pastors and leaders from other churches watched, hoping to pattern future transitions on what would occur, but found little to follow, as this move proved only minimally successful. Though the church has since gone forward and grown in number and influence, both men are tainted from the failure in their relationship and injured by the process. W...ho knows how many congregants harbor wounds of hurt and betrayal as well.

This brief narrative (while true, the names have been changed) is very indicative of both a current *and* increasingly encroaching problem throughout the United States and other countries. Some estimates suggest that one in six Protestant clergy quit the ministry every year. The United States has 350,000 ministers—but 50,000 leave the ministry annually.[1] According to statistics presented at a Leadership Network Succession Conference on March 26, 2013, close to sixty thousand churches go through leadership transitions each year.[2] With an aging baby-boomer population in the United States, one can only anticipate the number of church transitions taking place in the next ten years will increase exponentially—and in other organizations as well.

CREATING A CULTURE OF HONOR

In his book, *Transformational Intelligence,* Dr. Joseph Umidi points out that our real call in life is to *create culture,* not simply worship culture or become a creature of culture. He goes on to state:

> "Every family, company, church, and community group is a candidate to model a creative approach to culture that maximizes the best in people and the potential of the culture to contribute to the uplifting of community and city. That maximization will require an intentional focus in our approach to transform the role of culture in our lives."[3]

The challenge then, for the predecessor/successor, is to create a type of culture that *only they* can create. An honorable design based on healthy

1 Umidi, Joseph *Confirming the Pastoral Call: A Guide to Matching Candidates and Congregations.* Grand Rapids, MI: Kregel Publications 2000 pp. 12-13

2 Vanderbloemen, William *Leadership Network Succession Conference,* via webcast online: http://churchleadersuccession.com first published March 26, 2013

3 Umidi, Joseph *Transformational Coaching: Bridge Building that Impacts, Connects, and Advances the Ministry and Marketplace.* Fairvax, VA: Xulon Press 2007 p 10

relationships, an intentional focus, and one that maximizes and brings out the best in each other. The goal is to embrace and steward the value of honor in every part of the successor relationship.

The *gift* of honor can transform a relationship—and that relationship can shift a culture. Honor is a relational or social term that identifies how people in any society evaluate one another. How we evaluate worth affects our attitude and behavior toward others. He further writes:

> "We need an upgrade of relational honor, a download of transformational behavior that will result in significance, productivity, loyalty, camaraderie, unity, identity, courage, and tenacity at home and work. In short, we need our home and work environments to become cultures of honor."[4]

The story we shared at the beginning of this chapter illustrates the lack of an honoring culture. The bottom line for a peace-filled succession and transition in an organization, is to use the art of order to create an atmosphere of honor. Two rules are necessary:

1.   The predecessor becomes the successor's greatest cheerleader!
2.   The successor continually honors the predecessor!

Let's unpack what this fundamental mindset means and how it's implemented years before any transition finally happens. The lack of honor in the relationship between John and Roger could be attributed to the fact that neither had an understanding of, or had taken the time to analyze, their emotional intelligence. In their natural humanity, both men had fears, uncertainty, doubts, anxieties, and insecurities about themselves and each other.

---

4   Umidi, p. 12

When these negative emotions flood the relational atmosphere between leaders and within the ranks of people impacted, communication goes awry, positive plans go amiss, and God's vision for the leaders and the organization goes askew. Integrity and honesty in relationships becomes frayed. Instead of unity of vision, a fractured perspective of the future emerges. Finally, hope for the leaders' and organization's success, growth, and prosperity turns into depression, despair, and disappointment. The outgoing leader sees the vision which planted and prospered the church or entity through the years, disappearing and replaced by an "upstart" or "Absalom" leader who is set on a program of "out with the old, in with the new."

UNDERSTANDING AND CREATING AN ATMOSPHERE OF HONOR

> *Who then is Paul, and who is Apollos, but ministers through whom you believed, as the Lord gave to each one? I planted, Apollos watered, but God gave the increase. So then neither he who plants is anything, nor he who waters, but God who gives the increase. Now he who plants and he who waters are one, and each one will receive his own reward according to his own labor.* (1 Corinthians 3:5-8)

Disunity, conflict, critical comparisons, disorder and dishonor were all evidenced in the Corinth church. An atmosphere of honor considers thoughts, feelings, and actions—all of which comprise an attitude or mindset. They also strengthen the chain of wider influence.

Paul is saying in this text that one must be very careful how he/she builds upon another's foundation. Honor recognizes and affirms how God is using leaders to build His Kingdom. A successor dishonors a former leader when he/she takes the predecessor's picture off the wall, pulls their books or messages out of the bookstore, or makes unkind comments about the other person's ideas or efforts. Such actions reflect emotional immaturity and insecurity. Likewise, the ego of the predecessor can certainly prevent them from praising and promoting the giftings and work of the incoming successor.

We have seen the importance of creating an atmosphere of honor with not only the predecessors and successors, but also including other leaders, front line staff, and in our area of church specialty, the congregants. Almost always, the senior leader must desire and set in motion the creation of an atmosphere of honor.

*What do we mean by an **atmosphere of honor**?*

The sitting leader's motivations must arise out of his/her own emotional intelligence. Drawing upon a maturity rooted in humility, self-confidence, affirmation and love of others. They must have a deep desire for a successor, the church or organization, and himself/herself to experience God's best for the future.

Honor begins with honoring God and extends to honoring others. God states, . . . *for those who honor Me I will honor, and those who despise Me shall be slightly esteemed* (1 Samuel 2:30).

Honor [*cabad*) is defined in *The Theological Wordbook of the Old Testament* as "be heavy, grievous, hard, rich, honorable, glorious."

To succeed, the leaders and laity in a church congregation or organizational structure, honor, praise, and glorify God.

When it comes to honoring one another, we can turn to Paul's admonition in Romans 12:10. *Be kindly affectionate to one another with brotherly love, in **honor** giving preference to one another.*

Honor [timh/] in *Louw and Nida's Greek-English Lexicon of the New Testament* is defined as "high price, esteem, special or high value." This atmosphere of honor includes thoughts, feelings, and actions that respect and lift others up while not seeking honor or glory for oneself.

HONOR . . .

- Glorifies and praises God.
- Respects parents, elders, and leaders.
- Lifts people up rather than putting them down.
- Sacrifices personal agendas for what God wants and others need.
- Esteems, loves, and affirms others.
- Recognizes that everyone has been created in the image of God.
- Replaces arrogance with humility.
- Equips servant leaders.

Leaders who honor God and others are often called servant leaders. They embody the mandate of Galatians 5:13, ...*through love serve one another.*

One who honors others esteems the dignity, worth, and value of others without expecting some return for self. Honoring our parents refers not just to biological parents but also spiritual fathers and mothers and those surrogate parents like teachers, leaders, bosses, mentors, and coaches who have taught us by word and deed what is right, civil, kind, and polite.

Branch Rickey comments, "It is not the honor you take with you, but the heritage you leave behind."

James Cash Penney writes, "Honor bespeaks worth. Confidence begets truth. Service brings satisfaction. Cooperation proves the quality of leadership."[5]

These words speak volumes to the character and virtue of honor that need to mark the relationship between predecessor and successor in a leadership transition. Accountability ensures an honorable design.

Look at the chart describing an atmosphere of honor. Use it as a checklist or self-evaluation tool. Ask others to evaluate you on a scale of one to five with five being the highest.

Honor is an agenda-killer. By that we mean personal agendas, self-aggrandizement, selfish gain, and self-preservation behaviors. All are both exposed and defused by an atmosphere of honor. Neither the predecessor nor the successor in honorable transition are concerned with what they want, only with what God wants for them, and how the congregation, staff, volunteers, families, or anyone else will be affected. Everyone's future prosperity—spiritually, emotionally, and materially—is considered. Honor is birthed in an attitude of humility:

> *Your attitude should be the same as that of Christ Jesus:*
>
> *Who, being in very nature God, did not consider equality with God something to be grasped, but made himself nothing, taking the very nature of a servant, being made in human likeness.*
>
> *And being found in appearance as a man, he humbled himself and became obedient to death — even death on a cross!*
>
> —Philippians 2:5-8 NIV

---

5 https://www.brainyquote.com/topics/honor

Discovering One's Ability or Inability to Honor

How does a leader planning for transition measure his/her own ability to honor God and others, and to create an atmosphere of honor? An organizational head can begin self-examination by using an excellent tool that assesses Emotional Intelligence.

Often, the first question we are asked when talking to a client about issues surrounding Emotional Intelligence and emotional health is, "Why does this matter?"

In an era where everyone could talk via computer to everyone else without the benefits of connection, empathy or open communication, our personal relationships have suffered a massive blow. But in this context, our human realities will matter more than ever. Massive change and upheaval are constants. Technical innovations and increasingly competitive environments are creating internal flux, more than ever before. Previously, people and leaders could successfully hide a hot temper or shyness, because of less visibility and liability, but now, competencies such as managing one's emotions, handling encounters well, teamwork and leadership, are watched for more than ever.

As the world changes, so do the traits required for us to excel. Daniel Goleman reminds us that "out-of-control" emotions can make even smart people stupid. But emotional competence has at its very heart two abilities each church leader desperately needs: *empathy*, which involves reading the feelings of others, and *social skills*, which allow for the correct handling of those feelings skillfully.

When we coach a client regarding emotional intelligence, we review the five basic elements that emotional intelligence is predicated on:

1.   self-awareness

2. motivation
3. self-regulation
4. empathy
5. skillfulness in relationships

We do this by assessing each leader—primarily the predecessor and successor—and then evaluating and addressing those in sub-leadership and influencer roles, when given the opportunity.

No other area of transition is so easily overlooked or unplanned for as Emotional Intelligence, except for perhaps, Financial Planning (which we will also address later). As we move to the next chapter, we want to examine more fully how to use the tools of Emotional Intelligence with leaders and those they influence, moving everyone toward a successful transition. But first, let's consider some very important questions to help you strengthen your chain of influence. At the end of most chapters, we will provide these types of questions for personal self-examination and also for some small group or leadership discussion.

ASK YOURSELF AND OTHERS . . .

- What does an atmosphere of honor look like?

- How is an atmosphere of honor being created and perpetuated in my life and among our people?

- What attitudes and actions are inhibiting honor in my life and in our organization?

- What steps could be taken to elevate Emotional Intelligence in our people prior to a leadership transition in our organization?

- What five things can I change or adjust to promote a legacy of honor before, during and after transition?

"Change is situational. Transition, on the other hand, is psychological. It is not those events, but rather, the inner reorientation or self-redefinition that you must go through to incorporate any of those changes into your life. Without a transition, a change is just a rearrangement of the furniture. Unless transition happens, the change won't work, because it won't take."

—William Bridges, *The Way of Transition: Embracing Life's Most Difficult Moments*

CHAPTER 2

THE POWER OF EMOTIONAL INTELLIGENCE

"Out of control emotions can make smart people stupid."

— Daniel Goleman

In any transition, even those that are planned well with all the bases covered such as timeline, documents, financials (compensations, pensions, severance, etc.) communications and vision implementation—the oft overlooked area is that of Emotional Intelligence (EI). Few leaders of churches or organizations are aware of or concentrate on emotional maturation, including on a personal level. Emotional intelligence should be considered in the leadership of the local body, and in the general membership of the church or organization itself. Missing this crucial component will cause disorder.

Countless institutions, small, medium, and large in membership and budget, have taken the due diligence to plan specifically for transition in the senior leadership, and yet those transitions failed because the step of monitoring emotional intelligence was missed. In these cases, either the predecessor was emotionally deficient in some area, or the successor was, or both.

Quite frankly, succession planning is the ultimate test for determining how leaders have developed. But mature discipleship in Christ (the most effective leadership style known to man) cannot be realized without emotional maturation—it is an indispensable element of influence. As such, it should be evident and present as a significant attribute in those wise enough to follow Jesus' leadership example—particularly at the senior level. This is especially true when it comes to the inherently emotionally-charged dynamic of transition at the highest position(s).

Daniel Goleman in his book, *Working with Emotional Intelligence* writes, "The rules for work are changing. We're being judged by a new yard stick: not just by how smart we are, or by our training and expertise, but also by how well we handle ourselves and each other."

A resume will offer a reader a long history of education preparation, job experience history, and other key quality metrics. But beyond calling on a reference personally for insight into a potential key leader, we rarely develop an understanding of the emotional maturity and depth a particular individual will bring to the institution's table. This oversight can and will most probably have a very detrimental impact on the success of any transition. Sustained honor and order are impossible without Emotional Intelligence.

Honoring God, the Predecessor & the Successor

Weese and Crabtree in *Elephant in the Boardroom: Speaking the Unspoken about Pastoral Transitions* write about this often-missed consideration:

> "When it comes to pastoral transition, leaders often stop leading. The end result is that the congregation is left with no alternative, but it experiences the triple whammy of emotional, "organic," and organizational change all at the same time. The church is a living,

breathing organism and experiences all the same emotions as an individual."

For churches and other groups in transition, too often, because of the emotional immaturity and unaddressed emotional components of the predecessor and successor, the organization is brought into a state of dis-honor. When this happens, churches who should be seen as God's representation of His grace and mercy on the earth, are viewed by the outside community as un-unified, in disarray, and worse, without serious leadership.

However, when the EI component is in place and addressed, as well as all the other necessary paradigms (many which we will look at in this book), the chances of a long-lasting, successful transition increase substantially. Order is balanced and God is then honored.

When acting emotionally mature, the predecessor and successor have created an ideal atmosphere that brings honor to God and the congregation or peers they serve and love. This then creates the character that is necessary and most pleasing to the Holy Spirit. Defections and transfers are minimized, gossip is almost eliminated, vision is strengthened, the institution becomes multi-generational, and the kingdom is advanced in that particular community. Its reputation remains intact and the chain of influence is unbroken.

WHY EMOTIONAL INTELLIGENCE

First, an honest assessment of EI helps the outgoing leader (predecessor) develop an awareness and understanding of the dynamics affected by his/her eventual transition from a senior leadership role. With good transformational coaching following such an assessment, the following areas can be addressed and answered:

- The predecessor's place in the organization following the transition (1st a place of honor vs. title or job function) and how the group or congregation he/she has served will see him/her and respond to him/her.

- The predecessor's new season and opportunities which need to be investigated, planned for, and executed towards. There is *life* after leading/influencing/pastoring/preaching.

- The predecessor's disposition and mindset towards the successor both presently and into the future.

- The predecessor's spouse and the new role he/she will assume as well.

- The predecessor's role as the #1 cheerleader of the new successor and his/her leadership team, and how to display and vocalize that paradigm.

Second, an honest assessment of EI helps the incoming leader (successor) develop and form an emotionally healthy approach to his/her new role that will aid in setting forth principles and actions related to his/her eventual succession into the senior leadership role.

With good transformational coaching following such an assessment, the following areas can be addressed and answered:

- The successor's place in the organization following the transition (a place of honor vs. title or job function) and how the group or congregation he/she will now serve will see him/her and respond to him/her (ex. 'he's not like our old pastor', or, 'new broom sweeps the old out').

- The successor's new season and opportunities which need to be investigated, planned for, and executed towards. This new role is not just about leading/influencing or pastoring/preaching.

- The successor's disposition and mind-set towards the predecessor both presently and into the future.

- The successor's spouse and the new role he/she will assume as well.

- The successor's role as the lead person for the whole congregation or group who honors the predecessor and the former leadership team, and how to display and vocalize that honor.

Lastly, emotional intelligence assessment (EI) will help both leaders develop and maintain a healthy emotional mindset during and after transition that cannot be interrupted or derailed by internal or external forces. A mindset that seeks to glorify and honor Christ and His people in everything that is done. This exemplifies order at its best. Call it a "going the extra-mile" approach.

WHAT IS EMOTIONAL INTELLIGENCE?

It is the development of a healthy emotional wellness through the practice of talking about feelings that arise during transition: anger, sadness, joy, mistrust, loss, self-esteem, insecurities, fears, etc., and selecting healthy behavioral expressions of those feelings. Much of this is accomplished by doing a complete and thorough assessment and following that assessment up by transformational coaching for ALL parties concerned. (But most importantly the predecessor and spouse, and successor and spouse should participate in the process, but this can also be extended to the leadership, sub-leadership, and other influential people and groups of people).

HOW TO KNOW EI IS PRESENT IN INDIVIDUALS

- They handle criticism without denial, blame, excuses or anxiety.
- They're open-minded.
- They're good listeners.
- They don't sugar-coat the truth.
- They quickly apologize when they're wrong.
- They have an innate ability to regulate themselves, manage other people, and achieve success.

EI is therefore designed to address the most frequently unaddressed component in leadership development for the purpose of making the individual (and then as a result the group) the "total" of how God created them.

The Center for Creative Leadership states that, "75% of careers are derailed for reasons related to emotional competencies, including inability to handle interpersonal problems; unsatisfactory team leadership during times of difficulty and conflict; or inability to adapt to change or illicit trust."

WHAT ARE YOU PLANNING FOR?

There are always going to be transition points where there are more intense interactions between people, making emotional intelligence especially crucial. These are usually transition points in the various stages of leader/congregational/peer relationships. There are two words that capture transitions within any human context, but certainly in the church and institutional context: these are "danger" and "opportunity."

Transition moments in any organization are loaded with points of danger and things can quickly go terribly wrong. New seasons and beginnings often will require that greater amounts of energy and enthusiasm be applied, but there can also be times when human emotions cause the whole process to get off to a bad start. There is an old saying which bears repeating here, "We don't get a second chance to make a first impression." Think about its meaning in light of leadership transition.

When the deep relationships that have developed over time are now confronted with change and transition—and sometimes a necessary breaking or reformatting of long held relationships—an emotionally immature leader can at a minimum miss the potential opportunities found in a transition. That same transition then becomes only a process that must be endured by everyone. This is far from an honorable or orderly design.

As challenging as it is to first establish deep relationships within a peer group or congregation and leadership team, closing out those relationships, or reformatting them, can be just as complex. When moving to another congregation or moving into a new phase of leadership, or moving into retirement, an influencer who just walks out of people's lives without a meaningful closure with them is going to leave many deeply wounded.

The downside of this emotional immaturity is that it sets the successor up for failure from day one. We cannot expect the group will ever again enter a deep relationship with a future leader if they have their heart continually broken by the way the former influencer(s) have terminated their relationship with them. We have offered a couple of case studies throughout this book where leaders and pastors have done just that—all with devastating results.

Are you planning on just a job change, or a title change, or a leadership change—all without benefit of planning or addressing the EI issues? If so, you are planning on a greater chance of failure in the transition—and the real possibility that the organization you say you love will not last into a second or third generation of longevity.

Or perhaps you're not planning at all. You don't want to face your increasing chronological age, or maybe financial issues keep you from planning anything. Too many leaders have died in the highest position of authority without a thought of a plan. The organization generally dies with them. All that work, all that toil, all those tears, all those joys—gone in an instant. That in itself is a plan, although a horrible one. Churches are particularly vulnerable.

In the next ten years, thousands upon thousands of pulpits will undergo a transition (60,000 per year according to Leadership Network Succession Conference of 2013) and yet the odds are that only about 20-25 percent will enjoy a successful and lasting transition.

"Transitions themselves are not the issue,
but how well you respond to their challenges!"

−Jim George

A DOOMED TRANSITION TURNED AROUND

The church was twenty-five years old and the founding pastor was considering retirement. It was his desire that his chosen successor take the church—but it was also his desire to stay involved with the church as its founding pastor and remain salaried. He contacted Seira Group to assist the church through the transition process.

After a starting date was established for the initial work, pre-meeting information, including financials, retirement goals, numerous forms and EI assessments were requested from the church. The information was received, reviewed, and processed.

Upon meeting with the lead pastor and his wife, we realized that unless a miracle occurred, the transition/succession approach they had in mind would more likely end in disaster. Before we could go forward in our efforts to guide them through successfully, we had to address and hopefully assist the church in creating an atmosphere of honor and order.

One of the problems we faced was the relationship between the lead pastor and his next-in-line. Two years prior, the lead pastor had attempted to turn the church over to his chosen successor. The conversation broke down when communication and personal offenses caused the desired successor to leave the area with his wife and children.

Fast forward to our meeting. The potential successor and his family had returned to take the church after some low-level healing and concessions had taken place. Still, there were some very tender feelings, and a few raw spots in the relationships.

Another obstacle concerned questions the eldership team had concerning the congregation's loyalty to the predecessor who was remaining in the church, and the successor who they had never served, but would now become the leader of the church. They knew that while the vision of the church might not change, the philosophy and focus of the ministry would shift from a very prophetic run model to an evangelistic one. They knew that the predecessor and the successor had two different philosophies of ministry.

The elders were willing to resign, but the predecessor knew that a big shift in leadership may threaten the spiritual and financial foundations of the church. Another false start at transition/succession could render irreparable damage to the church. The elders were ready to serve the successor at his pleasure, but needed to know what his expectations of them would be. They also did not want their long relationship with the predecessor to in any way cause issues with security or loyalty concerns with the successor. They knew transition was needed but were concerned about becoming pitted between a predecessor and successor, should they continue their service as elders. They were conflicted.

Another obstacle they needed to overcome were the feelings that the successor and his wife held toward the predecessor and his wife.

> The predecessor and his wife wanted to stay in the church, while the successor and his wife wanted them to leave. Why?
>
> The negative experiences from the past had left the successor and his wife feeling they could never lead the church, with the predecessors' approval. They felt as if the predecessors would vicariously try to lead the church through them.

The successor also felt that the predecessors viewed his wife as a "work in progress" who needed to submit to them for mentoring and guidance. The Emotional Intelligence assessments showed that the emotional maturity was at a level that made working through the issues appear dim indeed. The EI assessments for each team member, including the predecessor and his wife and the successor and his wife, had also been sent to:

- a close friend outside the church
- a co-worker
- and a friend inside the church

Each was to complete the assessment with the appropriate team member in mind. This information enabled us to see how each person assessed themselves as opposed to the views of the people closest to them.

The differential between their friends' assessments and their own personal analysis helped us measure the quality of their public projection and communication accuracy. It is always difficult when the closest people in our sphere of influence interpret what we are projecting or communicating much differently than we intend. In transition, proper communication is factual, intentional, clear, and motivational.

In the case of this particular church, multiple meetings were required, careful explanation of the assessment results needed, and much prayer important, to bring all leadership members to a place of unity. The work was arduous, but after much soul-searching and working through some blind spots, offenses were addressed, forgiveness was asked for and received, and a fresh prospective was gained. This wonderful work was sealed by a sense of the Holy Spirit's guidance and favor. As a result, we were able to:

- assist them in drawing boundaries lines
- define a twenty-year vision
- build two-year benchmarks to measure progress
- assign roles
- align the congregation and ministries to the vision
- create assessment tools to help them stay on course
- help the leaders plan communication timelines as the transition plan developed through its phases
- assist them in planning to financially secure their future through monetarily honoring the outgoing pastors in a way the church could afford

Successful transitions culminate in a church planning and executing their leadership changes with honor, order, balance and dignity, that otherwise, would have likely ended in disaster. Without the EI component, true success cannot be achieved.

Dale Carnegie states it in the most benevolent way. "When dealing with people, remember you are not dealing with creatures of logic, but with creatures of emotion."

It's good to understand that increasing one's Emotional Intelligence is not easy. It does take some hard work over a long period of time. But consider how enriched organizational contemporaries and congregations are when they are led by emotionally intelligent, spiritually mature leaders. When proven strategies are followed, these organizations and churches become communities of healing and places where exciting things are taking place, where mission and ministry are advanced.

Even the emotional process of transition becomes an exciting adventure for the group and its leaders when every necessary success step is taken. An emotionally intelligent leader will remain a calm, confident, non-threatened presence in the midst of sometimes infantile actions of their people. They are able to deal with the inevitable conflicts that arise during transition and guide their group to a satisfying conclusion.

The emotional competencies of senior leaders, pastors, and their spouses are probably the most important factors in assuring a smooth transition between changing leadership. The very definition of emotional intelligence is the ability to control one's emotions without putting an impediment on them, while still using emotions constructively to achieve desired goals and to form strong, positive outcomes. Healthy emotional intelligence makes an honorable design possible, allowing for order in generational transition.

For example, knowing ahead of time that transition can be a highly-charged emotional journey for a close-knit church or organization, approaching the transition moment by allowing positive expressions of emotions from people who are feeling emotional about the event, helps to bring health and continuity to the organization. One significant sign of healthy emotional intelligence shows up in the form of optimism. Not just optimism alone, but with a confidence that is rooted in God's care for everyone concerned.

LEADING LIKE JESUS

When one examines Jesus' emotional intelligence, it is clear He had a deep understanding of His people. His was not a disembodied proclamation that He came to make, but one that responded to the deepest needs of His people. This was possible because of His emotional intelligence.

In short, your transition should be marked as one of the high-points or significant moments in the history of your church or organization.

Yes, it will be emotional, yes, it will mark some significant and sometimes uncomfortable or challenging changes, and yes, it will confront the status quo. But, it will also plant a transition point that will bring a new season of growth and health to the organization or church, particularly when the predecessor and successor are emotionally mature and healthy.

ASK YOURSELF AND OTHERS . . .

- Are the chief leader, staff, and lay leaders willing to honestly assess the EI of all directly impacted and playing a role in the process, beginning with the lead pastor in a church setting or the highest ranked authority in an organization? If so, what process and timeline will be set in place for doing so. If not, why not?

- Will the entire leadership team honestly share their feelings about transition, and if so, who will effectively facilitate that disclosure process?

- As the person reading this book, assess the strength of each feeling you are having about transition: (0 – not at all; 1 – slightly; 2 – somewhat; 3 – mildly; 4 – strongly; 5 – very intensely)

___ Anxious	___ Hopeful
___ Fearful	___ Confident
___ Despairing	___ Insecure
___ Calm	

In your planner, journal, or other private source of documentation, can you pinpoint why you feel so strongly about each emotion above that is marked with a 4 or 5?

Here's an exercise that may help bring further clarity to your thoughts and feelings right now.

- In the book, *Friend to Friend,* J. David Stone and Larry Keefauver suggest asking one's self three critical questions when working on a problem or decision:

  1. *What do you want for you?*
  2. *What are you feeling about what you want?*
  3. *What are you doing about it?*

Ask yourself these questions at least three times, answering differently each time. This helps you go beyond the presenting problem to identify some of the deeper issues you feel.

The authors also suggest you do this process with a trusted friend who will keep you honest and truthful in the process. When you have gone through the questions three times, then answer this:

  1. *What are you going to do about it?*
  2. *When will you do it?*
  3. *How will you do it?"*

A second set of questions can now be processed:

- *What does God want for you?*
- *What is God feeling about you and your situation?*
- *What does He want you to do?*
- *Will you do it—when and how?*

How do your answers to these questions line up with the first set of questions?

"The art of communication is the language of leadership."

—James Humes

"Any problem, big or small, within a [*church*] family, always seems to start with bad communication. Someone isn't listening."

— Emma Thompson

CHAPTER 3

THE PURPOSE OF EFFECTIVE, RESPECTFUL AND KIND COMMUNICATION

"The single biggest problem in communication is the illusion that it has taken place."

—George Bernard Shaw

When discussing honorable transitional design as it relates to communication, we must first assume that the Senior Leader—the one spearheading the transition and all its details—is not afraid to communicate. He/she must be committed to providing ongoing information to all parties involved and remain cognizant that all humans naturally require communication. In other words, senior leaders and the people who follow them, don't like surprises. They desire to "be in the know."

Regarding transitional honor and order, it's incumbent upon the leader(s) to understand the need for proper and timely communication, to pre-determine when communication is to happen, pre-determine who (various influence groups) receives communication, and to what depth each group is communicated with.

Too often it has been our experience that senior leaders and pastors can be the least attentive to the communication needs of his/her subordinates, and more importantly, to his/her members or congregation. In churches, we have observed cases where transition was communicated as late as the Sunday morning it was happening, with disastrous results. On the other side of that paradigm, we have observed that pitfalls occur when too much information is communicated too early, leading to confusion, opinions from everyone, and a sense of non-direction when it comes to the ongoing vision of the institution.

The ramifications of this not only produce a greater chance of turmoil within but can create a perception to the outside community of unprofessionalism. A "novice" or "rookie" mentality, regarding those who are leading the organization results.

Rollo May, a noted psychologist, states, "Communication leads to community, that is, to understanding, intimacy and mutual valuing."

This quote should be the goal of all strategic communication by the leader of any organization. When it comes to the issues of succession planning, how we communicate, and the goal we have attached to our communications, should produce the very values that May speaks of.

Communication, when done well and timed right, will bring understanding, and understanding will cause harmonious mutual relationships which can establish peace and stability in the church or organization. Communication should bring everyone on board and leave no one behind.

I'M STEPPING DOWN—NOW WHO DO I CALL?

Pastors and leaders do a lot of different things throughout their career, and they get very good at what they do. However, when it comes to transition and succession planning, they typically have never led a congregation or a leadership team through such an endeavor. Many probably have only a limited number of friends who have done so (most, not successfully). For most churches that are nondenominational in structure and Holy Spirit-led in function, calling for outside help, especially from someone with the label of "consultant" can be intimidating, or viewed as not necessary. These thoughts and mindsets then prejudice the leader from calling on the very professionals that can be the most helpful and provide the greatest chance of a successful outcome.

Why would anyone not seek outside professional help when it comes to one of the most potentially dangerous and critical moments in any church or organization's history?

Think about it . . . after years of blood, sweat, tears and toil, one of the most momentous decisions and moments in the entity's history is left to chance and unidentified external and internal forces to determine the course of action.

Calling a professional is NOT an admission of weakness, nor is it a deliberate slighting of the Holy Spirit. The wise leader recognizes his or her weakness, lack of knowledge, or even fear, when it comes to handling such a delicate and exceptionally significant event.

To Tell or Not to Tell—That is the question

Because of the uncertainty of a leader, or to the other extreme, the pride and arrogance of some leaders who think they have this "transition" thing all figured out—some who have been mostly successful in the founding of and building up of a local church, have in just a few hours, destroyed all they worked to obtain. Poor timing, confusing communication, and unwise discernment of the people have led so many down the same path to ruin.

The extreme of far too much secretiveness concerning transition endangers an organization undergoing leadership change. But spewing forth information and ideas and what-ifs to anyone who will listen is equally perilous. Both of these scenarios will very likely insure a complete failure of the transition—wounding many people in the process. Take the following true story as an example.

A MOMENTOUS DECISION

Pastor Doug had founded his church 28 years prior to the night of his leadership board meeting. He had raised up a great ministry, where his children grew and many of them served the Lord in various ministries—one of them with him at his church. He had also successfully equipped many other leaders who were sent out to pioneer their own churches, and because of this, he led a great network of pastors that looked to him as an apostolic father. His key leaders were at this meeting, several who were pastoring some of his satellite churches in and around the city; although up to this point, he remained the senior pastor of all those churches. He intended to let them all know of his intention to step aside and transition out of the pastoral leadership, naming his son as his successor.

Early in the meeting, attitudes and emotions deteriorated as he stated his plan to step down. His announcement caught everyone unaware, especially when he admitted to the board he had spoken to no one prior to this meeting about his momentous decision. The problem was multiplied when he also announced that he would "cut" loose a couple of the satellite churches from the mother church, so they could go it alone with their leaders. When he divulged that his son would take over the mother church, the problem was further compounded.

Unfortunately, not even the son was aware of this decision beforehand and was caught totally unprepared. During the ensuing weeks, the church verged on total collapse. The pastor's own immediate family suffered great stress, the elders and other pastors of the satellite churches all felt disenfranchised for no good reason. His son felt betrayed and conflicted because he had not been consulted.

A church of several thousand, built up wonderfully and powerfully over many decades, was about to crash and burn because of the simple lack of honor and order in communication. Later, the son and father tried to bring everyone, including the satellite leaders, back into the fold without success. It was too late. They had been wounded beyond measure, and the son was now left to try and restore a name and a network, with very little help and resources.

The church eventually made a turn-around. The son went on to pastor and work with his father, while the satellite churches gained their own strength and saw the division healed as best as possible. But none of this should have happened—and could have been prevented.

EFFECTIVE COMMUNICATION IS:

- Clear
- Confronting–speaks the truth in love
- Consistent
- Continual
- Collaborative–dialogue not just monologue
- Caring

This was poor communication in the extreme, with a good dose of a lack of discernment thrown in. This pastor had always operated with a "word" from the Lord and had expected the followers to just follow. He did not realize that people leading under his authority expected better communication than this. They expected an orderly process, to be informed of the details, and to be gently treated and sold on the value of such a drastic change of direction. They expected to be consulted and allowed to express their opinions, with consideration given to their thoughts, even if they were not acted upon. They were, after-all, co-leaders. Most importantly, they expected to be treated with honor—their expectations were reasonable.

WHEN SHOULD THEY KNOW? TIMELINE OF COMMUNICATION

As seen in the above case study, this pastor thought the elder meeting was the perfect time to make his announcement. After all, he had thought about this decision long and hard for a good length of time. However, he failed to understand that he was dealing with people's lives and livelihood, and those affected by his decision were blindsided—they had been given no time to ponder, consider, or get used to the potential change.

For instance, his son should have been approached privately, long before this meeting, to add his input into the decision, following his own determination by the Holy Spirit that he "was the one." After that was accomplished, the other satellite pastors should have been individually approached, as well. Communicating the whole matter to the group on a "prayer" level, well before this meeting and "final" decision, should have happened as a first step. This orderly format would have made everyone affected feel as if they were honored and part of the process.

Most leaders have never had to communicate something as vital and critical to the organization's ongoing health, as details concerning succession. They recognize and fear that most people don't want to hear what they must say on the matter. Change brings out human nature at its rawest. We all like things to stay the same.

Additionally, most leaders are not fully aware that everyone in his/her institutional body has a great desire to be on the "inside" of every news item. Succession planning is no different. The truth is, everyone has an opinion. How a leader successfully navigates the communication leg of succession planning will make all the difference to the people he/she serves, and the level of buy-in received. Within any organization, there are always several levels and layers of various influencing groups. A good leader will be fully aware of this and manage the communication appropriately.

INTERNAL COMMUNICATION (ORGANIZATION) AND EXTERNAL COMMUNICATION (COMMUNITY)

Another important factor to consider, as it relates to succession and transition, is the balance and approach of communication to both the organization and community. Depending on the size of the entity and the size of the community—all aspects being relative—a good leader will make communication with the community an equally high a priority to his/her communication within the institution. The way the news of pending transition is managed can always affect (positively) the community in which the organization engages.

If the communication is approached positively, and if potential questions about the transition are answered prior to the questions being verbalized, transition can prove to have many positive benefits to that local entity and its reputation in the community. Positive communication provided at the right time in the right way where an organization resides, is another aspect of honor.

Honor the community by including them—not in the decision-making—but certainly by alerting them to the decision itself. Once this is done, at a minimum it witnesses to the health and longevity of your organization, within your home community. Always remember, people normally don't like change and will by default try to resist it. However, if change is inevitable, they like to see order and continuity, and want to be included in your communications.

This is especially true if you are a church and have been actively engaged in ministry in and to the community prior to the transition. Depending on the size of the community and church, it is even sometimes appropriate to let city fathers/leaders personally know of your impending changes. Get them on board. This speaks well of your church and its community interface.

ASSESSING THE VERACITY OF ALL COMMUNICATIONS

This very simple concept is steeped in honor. It's not only talking, but making sure with appropriate and specific feedback, that what you are communicating is being heard in the right way. Nothing feeds the grapevine better than good gossip you as a leader helped to unwittingly develop by lack of or unclear communication.

One of our clients knew ahead of time that he would encounter resistance to transition from his older generation, who had walked with him from the beginning. In wisdom, he met with that older group alone (once the transition decision had been made by the leadership). During the evening's dinner, where he honored them and their service, he shared his heart for the next generation of younger leaders (not his heart to retire or leave the ministry). He made sure the mature generation "bought in" to "helping" him make the next guy successful.

The wonderful effect of this approach was the reaction whenever any of the older generation who were at that night's dinner heard anyone (young or old) questioning or complaining about the "new guy." When it happened, they stopped and reprimanded gossip, and helped to bring naysayers on board, in support of the transition.

Leaders don't seem to fully understand: Sheep birth sheep, *but also,* sheep talk to sheep!

COMMUNICATING VISION FOR THE FUTURE

It should be obvious that all communication about the transition should primarily pertain to the "future" and "ongoing vision" of the body. It is not a time for senior leaders to talk about their retirement, or getting to move to a wonderful geographical location, etc. Everyone's probably happy for the retiring influencer, but they don't want to hear all the detailed plans.

"Their future" and the "organization's new leadership" is foremost on the minds of those who will deal with the transitional after-effects. They want to hear that the entity in which they have invested their time, talent, and monies in (the vision) is going to continue and expand.

Prior to, and during the transition season, provides the very best time to plan a series of messages on future, vision, expansion, on the next thing etc. This should, of course, be coordinated with the successor, and perhaps be a joint approach.

Talk of vision and future is necessary at this stage more than ever before, particularly if key areas are going to be re-aligned, or personnel (other than the two primary players) are going to be reassigned. Make sure everything coming out of your lips is filled with faith and encouragement concerning the future of the Kingdom of God, the organization, the local church and ministries, and the people involved and committed to the process.

ASK YOURSELF AND OTHERS . . .

What are your leadership's communication strengths?

- Clear
- Confronting—speaks the truth in love
- Consistent
- Continual
- Collaborative—dialogue not just monologue
- Caring

Rank in order the above strengths from the strongest to the weakest. Then after each communication quality, write down how to further strengthen that quality in the transition process at your organization and within the entity's leadership.

"A ministry organization's core values are at the center of its corporate culture . . .

A church's core values are a vital part of its character, which is also determined by its mission, vision, and strategy."

— Aubrey Malphurs, *Values-Driven Leadership*

CHAPTER 4

THE PRIMACY OF CORE VALUES

"Civilization ceases when we no longer respect and no longer put into their correct places the fundamental values, such as work, family and country; such as the individual, honor and religion."

— R.P. Lebret, *Defining Values*

The word "values" has many meanings depending on the context in which it is used. Webster states that one possible meaning for the word is, "something (such as a principle or quality) intrinsically valuable or desirable."

The use of the word "values" in this chapter refers to "commonly held attitudes, beliefs, and characteristics which constitute the core of what is important to a healthy organization." Values undergird order and honor.

Values are the principles that determine the direction of any thriving entity. Our values also influence behavior and mission, helping to determine not only what is done, but also how we go about accomplishing our goals. Our values then, become the foundation for determining what is most important.

THE IMPORTANCE OF VALUES

When you drive through many of the cities in America, you may be struck by their skylines. Often, city skylines are used to promote the tourism industry on television, social media outlets, and magazines. New York, Chicago, L.A., and Boston are perhaps the most famous for their aerial view architecture, but there are many other cities around the world that have spectacular skylines as well. It's amazing to look at them and realize that before any of those gigantic buildings came into physical existence, they were first a thought that when shared with a planner, became a blueprint. When contracted with a construction company, the blueprint became a reality after a foundation was laid, upon which the building was constructed.

The foundation of the Empire State Building in New York City was started in 1929. The building is constructed in such a way that it sways some five feet at the top and has been doing just that since its completion in December of 1931. Can you imagine the amount of pressure applied to its foundation?

Without a solid well-constructed foundation, the building would not last. In this sense, the foundation is the most important part of the building. It holds and stabilizes the entire structure, including the elemental pressures applied on it by the forces of nature. Likewise, core values are essential to the structural integrity of your church or organization—and your personal life. When there are no values to support, guide, and provide the basis for decision-making, your life and the life of your church or organization will not stand against the pressures exerted upon it.

In transition, it is important that the predecessor understands that the successor will bring new thoughts, ideas and methodology concerning the future of the body she/he represents. It is equally as important that the successor understands the core values (foundation) upon which the body was built, and maintains a strong fidelity to those values.

The Apostle Paul refers to this principle when he cautions a new generation of ministers to be careful how they build upon another man's foundation.

"Because of God's grace to me, I have laid the foundation like an expert builder. Now others are building on it. But whoever is building on this foundation must be very careful. For no one can lay any foundation other than the one we already have—Jesus Christ. Anyone who builds on that foundation may use a variety of materials—gold, silver, jewels, wood, hay, or straw. 13 But on the judgment day, fire will reveal what kind of work each builder has done.

The fire will show if a person's work has any value. 14 If the work survives, that builder will receive a reward. 15 But if the work is burned up, the builder will suffer great loss. The builder will be saved, but like someone barely escaping through a wall of flames."[6]

CORE VALUES ARE . . .

- essential to the structural integrity of your organization and your personal life.
- important for the successor to understand that they are the (foundation) upon which the church or entity was built and to maintain a strong fidelity to those values.
- necessary for the successor to build upon, including the spiritual, theological, and social history of the church or organization, and the hermeneutic of its past.

---

6 Tyndale House Publishers, *Holy Bible: New Living Translation* (Carol Stream, IL: Tyndale House Publishers, 2013), 1 Cor. 3:10–15.

Eugene Peterson renders the previous passage this way:

> *"Or, to put it another way, you are God's house. Using the gift God gave me as a good architect, I designed blueprints; Apollos is putting up the walls. Let each carpenter who comes on the job take care to build on the foundation! Remember, there is only one foundation, the one already laid: Jesus Christ. Take **particular care** in picking out your building materials. Eventually there is going to be an inspection. If you use cheap or inferior materials, you'll be found out. The inspection will be thorough and rigorous. You won't get by with a thing. If your work passes inspection, fine; if it doesn't, your part of the building will be torn out and started over. But you won't be torn out; you'll survive—but just barely".*[7]

The succession planning and transition process presents some of the same concerns that Paul addressed 2,000 years ago. His concern was that the leader after him (the successor) understood that he was working on a project that was another person's work. The architect had produced a blueprint that was used to lay the foundation. The construction company needed to carefully follow the architect's drawings, to choose materials that met the engineer's specs, and the building completed exactly according to design. The finished structure would be what the foundation was designed to carry. These orderly steps would ensure longevity and strength.

Every successor needs to understand the spiritual, theological, and social history of the organization or church, and the hermeneutic through which it was filtered. Only then will the successor understand the present stance of the body they represent, and the opportunities

---

7 Eugene H. Peterson, *The Message: The Bible in Contemporary Language* (Colorado Springs, CO: NavPress, 2005), 1 Cor. 3:15.

and challenges ahead. They must navigate wisely, to position those they lead for a healthy embrace of any change in the vision for the future. The successor must realize that he is building on someone else's foundation, and his own body of work will serve as the foundation of his/her successor on a day in the future.

Successors must be careful, they must be wise. Remember, our values are our foundation, and our foundation sustains our strength!

The late Dr. Martin Luther King Jr. said, "If we are to go forward, we must go back and rediscover those precious values—that all reality hinges on moral foundations and that all reality has spiritual control."

VALUES MATTER

Organizations may attract all kinds of people with different values. If the mission is not clearly articulated through its values from the beginning, bringing a sense of unity, the entity can be pulled apart by chaos in its diversity.

Most strategic planning fails due to lack of values articulation early enough in the process. If core values are not established, clear direction is also difficult to establish, and a lack of order takes root.

Ultimately, we prioritize our time, energy and money according to our values. It is wise to clarify your personal values and the core values of your mission, then prioritize your time to live out those values. If you are unclear about what your core values are, and unfamiliar with how to formulate them, coaching in this area will provide great benefit for you.

Values are the ideals and core beliefs we are passionate about, because they communicate your primary standards. A belief is a conviction or opinion you hold to be true. Values are non-negotiable and must be lived out in daily practice. When clarified, articulated, and lived out consistently, values keep us on track. Communicating values must precede moving forward with vision, because vision is built on the foundation of your values. Values are the glue that bonds the team to each other and its mission.

CORE VALUES

> *"It's not hard to make decisions*
> *when you know what your values are."*
>
> –Roy E. Disney

A church's primary values are defined as its unceasing, fervent, scriptural core principles that guide, guard, and govern its ministry. This definition has important key elements.[8] And these crucial insights are important considerations for any entity in transition.

- **Core values are perpetual.** Core values change very slowly. This is why it is hard to revitalize an established organization. It takes a substantial length of time to change group values. Consequently, it's critical to begin with the right standards.
- **Core values are enthusiastic.** *Vision* is a seeing word; *enthusiasm* is a feeling word. Core values are heartfelt and elicit strong emotions. They stir feelings that can move people to biblical, Christ-honoring quests.
- **Core values are based in scripture.** The true test of an intrinsic values statement comes from asking yourself, *Is it rooted in Scripture?* While it may not necessarily be found in the Bible, it should be rooted in Scriptural principles.

---

8 Malphurs, Aubrey, Values Driven Leadership: *Discovering and Developing Your Core Values for Ministry* Baker Books, Grand Rapids MI. 49516; 1996, p 34.

- **Values are core convictions.** Values are your core convictions. A conviction is a deep-seated opinion or belief you hold to be true based on limited evidence.
- **Values guide, guard and govern the ministry.** Values are deeply ingrained convictions that inform and direct how decisions are made, money is spent, risks are taken, problems solved, goals set, and priorities determined.[9] This is true for any organization's mission.

In transition, the predecessor and successor should place the clarity of values very high on their priority list, because values are the foundation upon which the future is built. The security and longevity of any vision cast for the future is sustained by the quality and strength of defined values.

The quality and strength of the foundation will determine the heights reached by the structure. The lead pastor and successor's ability to work together to bring clarity of values into the initial planning of the transition/succession process, exponentially increases the chances the successor's vision of the future will succeed.

The successor must learn to lead the organization forward with Godly wisdom, sticking with an adherence to its fundamental values.

William Bridges, in writing about business transitions states, "Never belittle the past. Many new leaders in their enthusiasm for a future that is going to be better than the past ridicule or speak mockingly of the old way of doing things. In doing so they consolidate the resistance against the transition because people identify with the way things used to be and thus feel their self-worth is at stake whenever the past is attacked."

---

9 Adapted from: *Values-Driven Leadership: Discovering and Developing Your Core Values for Ministry* by Aubrey Malphurs.

Applying this statement to the church, non-profit, family owned business, or other organization, *the successor must resist the temptation to lead the entity away from its DNA or the value system it has been built on.*

VALUE ALIGNMENT

After the core values of the institution are defined and identified, there must come to that organization an alignment and implementation of those core values into every element and sub-mission or sub-ministry.

Perhaps it's helpful to think of it this way: *Have you ever driven a car that had a tire out of balance or had an alignment issue?*

An unbalanced tire produces a wobble and a bump when traveling. An alignment issue causes the car not to track correctly and to pull or veer to the left or right.

Usually, when new tires are put on a car, the tires are first "balanced" on the wheel by spinning the tire at a high speed, then adding weights to the wheel rim until there is no longer a wobble in the tire as it spins. The car travels without bouncing.

For alignment, when new tires are put on a car, it is placed on a lift to align the front tires with the rear tires. This allows the car to track correctly when traveling and it doesn't veer to the right or left. When the tires are balanced and properly aligned, driving the car, even at high speeds, is a pleasure—and as the driver, you are not fighting a "pull."

Unified missions or ministries are no different. Each team member of your leadership, each staff member, every ministry or department leader (volunteer or paid), is balanced by the weight of the organization's values. When the core values are understood, adopted and applied by the entire leadership as personal and corporate non-negotiables, the foundation for vision fulfillment is solidly in place. The journey becomes smooth and pleasurable.

When core values are *not* the same across the leadership spectrum, the mission becomes bumpy, wobbly, slow, arduous and disappointing. The team's lifespan is also significantly reduced.

Succession planning is a great place to assess the "values balance and alignment" so at the eventual transition point, the successor can begin to lead further down the road without conflict, disorder, or confusion. It is comforting to know that the entire leadership is unified and there is no drag placed on the church, ministry, organization, business, or mission. The group continues to "track" successfully, even down to the smallest departmental component. Maximum traction is achieved, momentum is not wasted or diverted, but is actually allowed to increase, and everyone on board enjoys a sense of comfort, security and peace during the ride.

VALUES DETERMINE CULTURE

Every ministry, every company and even every home has a core set of values; and those values, when affirmed and lived out, result in a corresponding culture. For example, a company that values strong customer appreciation and service will exhibit and build a culture where the customer is highly respected and treated well. Additionally, a customer who feels they are highly valued, will honor that company with their continued business, and will even tell their friends and family about that company. They inherently want to share with others the culture of that company.

The same thing applies to churches, ministries, and nonprofits. They gather and gain strength because of the culture produced by a set of core-values. If culture is developed without value or foundational moorings—in other words, culture is only created to produce a short term feeling or mood, or to appease a changing societal culture—they endanger themselves. When another church, ministry, or nonprofit down the street produces a better feeling or mood (culture), or the society ascribes to a new cultural mood, the organization is going to bounce all over the place—producing no fruit or "long-term" generational commitment.

Culture following can often produce quick results, but hardly ever produces sound and permanent change in people's lives. Beware: *this way of fitful living sometimes seems to produce the right or holy results we are seeking, but it's a temporary illusion.*

Ultimately though (if the lack of strong values and foundations doesn't show consequences in your life), they will certainly show up in the next generation. Many societies today are in turmoil around the world, because we have become very good and fond of following the next best thing (culture) and have no time or use for foundations and values.

Jack Hayford has been quoted as saying he never set out to produce a "great church" (culture-driven), but to produce a "great people" (value-driven). What he describes takes time, but more importantly, it takes a continual fidelity to the values designed to guide your life and the lives represented in your people.

AN EXAMPLE OF VALUES DISHONORED, LEADING TO A CHANGED CULTURE

As a conclusion to this important chapter, we want to offer a true story of a ministry that failed to understand and hold true to its core values. This does not represent an isolated case in our current global culture or in the church world, but sadly, is happening with more frequency. The results are proving disastrous. Disastrous, not just to the ongoing viability of one local church, but to a society and culture the church was designed to lovingly confront.

COLLAPSE OF CORE VALUES

The church had established a long history and reputation for being a spirit-centered presence, welcoming, offering Bible teaching fellowship, and remaining committed to producing strong disciples who were influencing and touching their community.

These attributes represented a strong core-value system. The church had already experienced one transition from the founder to the first successor, and that successor had enjoyed a long and fruitful ministry which produced growth, stability, and influence in so many lives.

Things began to fall apart soon after the church transitioned to the third generation. A few years into his leadership, the successor began to feel dissatisfied with the steady, solid and smooth growth the church had always enjoyed. He began instead, to turn the church to a more attractional-based ministry. Consequently, this inevitably required a departure from the strong Spirit-sensitive worship service, as well as strong biblical preaching and teaching people were used to.

Now, the worship was more a spectator-centered event, and the biblical teaching of principles and disciplines was limited to the occasional class or seminar. The overwhelming "new" core value became, "do not offend, convict, or challenge" by word, deed or action.

Amazingly, and to be expected, the church grew at an astounding pace. Its influence and stature also increased at an accelerated pace. It soon became one of the mega-churches in this mega-city. Because of its growth success, it quickly gained a very well-known reputation in its nation and around the world.

Make no mistake, this wasn't just a change in methodologies. This wasn't choosing to sing choruses as opposed to hymns or reading from the New King James Version as opposed to the old King James. This was a deliberate and planned shift from pre-established core-values, and the ignoring and rejecting of those values, which in turn created a new culture.

The problem was, the foundations of the old values, and the culture it produced, had kept the church true and faithful to its vision and mission for decades. It had not wavered or varied for two succeeding generations, but now a third generation had decided to make a change to the very fundamental DNA of the church. The result brought confusion, disillusionment, a loss of identity, and ultimately a "counter-culture" to the one first established in the church.

It began with small little turns, a watering down of the preached Word, a race for greater innovations in worship and presence, that left the congregation behind, while the expert musicians honed their talents. Finally, in order to attract even more people, larger turns had to be made and compromise was required in several sensitive and debatable areas (alcohol stance, LGBTQ acceptance, etc.). It was over before it was officially over. Soon a great split came into the church between those who were progressive and those who desired a return to God honoring values. In the middle of this the pastor was asked to step down by the leadership, having now lost his authority and mandate to lead effectively. He had not provided a clear and uncompromising set of values to the next generation, and without it he was no longer pastoring – just 'community organizing.'

Values and DNA that had built and kept the church ministering effectively over many decades, now denigrated to a large church with an empty heart, and its identity lost. It wasn't that a large church was such a wrong goal—most churches desire growth and new converts. In this case, in order to achieve the growth, the only way forward was "man's way." The leadership discovered like Adam and Eve, the apple on that tree seemed so delicious and fulfilling—until you took a big bite.

Unless you are fully aware *all the time* of the attack on your values, you will lose the greater battle. (You can lose within your country or city, within your business, within the church you attend and serve, even within your family.)

Values create the "culture" of the organization. Culture is formed as the core values permeate the hearts and minds of the leadership and followers. Culture is evidenced in the lifestyle and practices of the people.

Again, these core values determine "who we are" and "what we are." Once these are answered, we can then move forward to one of the most asked questions in succession planning and transition moments, which is, "Where we are going as a church, organization, entity, group, etc.?" That leads us to the next chapter on Vision Alignment.

ASK YOURSELF AND OTHERS . . .

- List and describe the core value of the head leader.

- List and describe the original core values of the organization at the time the head leader planted the work or took the leadership position.

- Compare the two lists. How are they the same and how are they different?

What is a vision?

Perhaps the best way to describe a vision, is as *a picture of a preferred future.* Rosabeth Moss Kanter believes that such a picture must be in place before people can let go of the past and permit change to take place.

As Aristotle put it, "The soul never thinks without a picture."

"A vision is a dream.
It is a picture of what is possible."

— Lovett H. Weems Jr., *Leadership Matters*

CHAPTER 5

The Productivity
of Vision Alignment

*If people can't see what God is doing, they stumble all over themselves; But
when they attend to what he reveals, they are most blessed.*

—Proverbs 29:18 MSG

The familiar King James Version text for Proverbs 29:18 reads,
"Where there is no vision, the people perish." We might adapt
this truth for churches and organizations and their leaders in transition
by affirming that, without a unified vision among leaders in transition,
the body will perish, divide, splinter, fail, or die. This is true for any
group dealing with a leadership change.

Honoring the Past, Present and Future

A successful transition requires a clear and accurate understanding of
an organization's history, present and future, to include its destination
and waypoints along the way. Public transportation would never have
a passenger if the taxi, subway, bus, train, ship or plane who did not
have a clearly visible destination displayed to provide order. The leader
who says about the immediate or distant future, "let's keep going and
see what happens," is certainly on a journey to nowhere. Remember

the dialogue between Lewis Carroll's Alice and the Cheshire cat, in *Alice in Wonderland*?

> "Cheshire-Puss," [said Alice], "would you tell me please, which way I ought to go from here?"
>
> "That depends a good deal on where you want to get to," said the Cat.
>
> "I don't care much where," said Alice, "so long as I get somewhere," she added as an explanation.
>
> "Oh, you're sure to do that," said the Cat, "if you only walk long enough."

Such a walk for a pastor, predecessor, successor, and other leaders, will often end up not in a leap of faith, but in a disastrous falling off a cliff. In his classic study on leadership, Professor Lovett Weems writes, "The capacity for preserving an organization, its values, and its mission lies in continuous renewal and regeneration. There is a simple and familiar cycle through which organizations tend to move: from initial vision to maintenance and decline.

In the early days, the vision is very pure and is the dominant characteristic of the organization. There is a passion about purpose and mission. Later comes a time when the organization takes on institutional characteristics, without which it could not continue to make significant cultural impact. However, in this stage there is enough distance from the initial vision that maintenance comes to the fore, and vision often wanes. Then, when the organization becomes cut off from its source of power, its initial purpose and vision, it moves into decline."[10]

Like other establishments, churches considering leadership transition

---

10 Weems, Lovett H. Jr. *Church Leadership: Vision, Team, Culture, and Integrity* Nashville, TN: Abingdon Press, 2010. pp. 22f.

must have a comprehensive transition/succession plan that clearly communicates where the church has been, where it is, and where it is going if it desires the congregation to get on board and the church to successfully transition into the future. This requires thought, analysis, reflection, inquiry, assessment, planning, projection, and most importantly, prayer and skillful communication. The Bible provides outlines and insights for doing this well.

God instructed the prophet Habakkuk to, *"Write down the revelation* [vision] *and make it plain on tablets so that a herald may run with it."* (Habakkuk 2:2 NIV)

"Write what you see. Write it out in big block letters so that it can be read on the run." (Habakkuk 2:2 MSG)

It is obvious from His instructions, that God's supports clear communication, especially important when a leadership change is imminent.

VITAL TO TRANSITION SUCCESS

Vision determines direction and narrows options; so vision will always lead to a strategic plan. Strategic planning leads to successful execution. The following account shows what happens when you unwisely try to recast the organizational vision, versus when you pursue an honorable design based on the art of order for generational transition.

WHERE TO TAKE THEM

A large and successful mega church in the upper Midwest was facing a bit of a crisis. After thirty years of faithful ministry and taking a small denominational church from years of narrow thinking to becoming a very significant church in the city, state and its denomination. The senior leader who had set such a vision for growth was burned out and knew he needed a change. Because of the parameters of that local church's government, the predecessor could gently suggest a replacement, but the ultimate decision would be made by the Board of Deacons.

The Pulpit Search Committee was established, resumes were collected, sermons were listened to as a means of audition; and, eventually, a list of several potential candidates was narrowed down to two or three. The Board hastily picked a new pastor from the West Coast to fill the pastoral position. Within very short order after his arrival, it became apparent that a huge mistake had been made. This church of many thousands of people began to see a significant and steady decline in people and finances that soon caused a glaring alarm to sound for everyone, including the new pastor.

He had come into this new Midwest environment with a brand-new vision and direction. He determined to change the very ethnic make-up of the church with deliberation and resolve, without any regard to its history or current culture. He firmly believed he was called to bring a massive philosophy shift in every area of the church, all without even understanding the city he had come to. This wasn't simply an evangelistic mandate, but literally a rejection of all its past and present. His fresh vision sounded noble and "kingdom like" when it was presented, but it was unwise at best and arrogant at worst—void of any honor.

Within two years, he had become totally frustrated with the people, and the people were frustrated with him. They were seeing all they had worked so hard to build and establish, including a sterling reputation, crumble like dust because of an unwillingness to invest time in study and understanding of the church's history, culture and its people. This mistake ended in the only possible outcome that could be expected—total failure (failure for the church's vision and purpose, failure for the people of the church, and failure for this senior leader).

Within four years, the successor had come and gone, and the process for a replacement was again initialized. This time, care was taken to find a candidate who in prior years had a relationship with the church, and who not only knew its history, but honored that history as he led them into their future.

Now, years later, the church is making a steady but slow comeback. It has had to regain its vision by remembering and honoring its past, while at the same time proving open to moving forward. This new pastor knew where to take them.

Did their successful transition include some cultural shift in the church? Absolutely! But the lesson learned by all was that it was unwise to dishonor people and culture by refusing to remember the past. Without that honoring of the past, and yes, the present and future, their vision was in danger of being lost or stolen.

ASSESS WHERE YOU ARE & WHAT YOU SEE?

If you are the senior leader considering transition, looking behind you is much clearer than gazing into the future. The future, however, is what you want to insure.

Safety, security, confidence in God's ongoing favor without you in the shepherding position, underpins the church or organization's success moving forward. Remember that favor is God being faithful to your faithfulness. It is also important that your body of work, (all the study, prayer, training, sermons, counseling, personal ministry, investment in people, and service to the community) serves as a springboard your successor can use to take the congregation or team to the next level. If you do your job correctly, your successor will excel, and his/her success will be greater than yours. This is called a WIN and becomes part of your legacy.

WHAT FROM THE PAST IS IMPORTANT TO THE FUTURE?

What you want to carry forward into the future is the parts of your history that are important to you and the people who are part of the mission, including how the organization was birthed, and the waypoints on the journey where God interacted or intervened in a supernatural way that everyone acknowledged.

These are the ancient landmarks that should never be removed. They are the twelve stones that Joshua commanded to be brought out of the Jordan River and stacked as a memorial. The purpose was to show future generations that God moves on the behalf of his people and brings them through the seeming impossibilities of life onto dry ground. (Joshua 4:4-9)

Therefore, just like Joshua of old, you as the leader must be at the front of all transition/succession planning, setting the pace, determining the direction and requiring accountability of all delegated tasks. This is done to assure the desired security and realization of the church's future, enabling it to accomplish its mission, long after you are gone.

In many ways, this may be the greatest contribution you will ever make in your ministry. Your impact will affect future generations, lasting long after you are gone.

DO THEY SEE WHAT YOU SEE?

The most basic ways businesses, nonprofits, other entities, and churches communicate vision is through written statements. Usually this includes statements of:

PURPOSE which answers the question, "Why does this organization exist?" Its orientation is philosophical, explaining the entity's reason for being.

VISION which answers the question, "What is the organization supposed to accomplish in the marketplace?"

Vision is "seeing" oriented. What do we think of or imagine when vision is communicated to us?

MISSION answers the question, "What is the organization's function?" Its orientation is objective, describing what our plan looks like.

VALUES answer the question, "Why do we do what we do?" Its orientation is reflective, setting the benchmarks that guide future decisions. They provide the needed boundaries each department or ministry needs.

PHILOSOPHY OF MINISTRY or SERVICE answers the question, "Why do we do what we do, the way we do it?" Its orientation describes values and communicates what shapes our organizational culture.

You may want to gather the core leadership of your organization and ask them to write a sentence defining each of the above statements. See the diagram on this page. When everyone has completed their statement definitions, collect all of them and discuss as a group how similar or dissimilar they are.

THE ORGANIZATION'S STATEMENTS

Ask the core leadership to complete these sentences.

Our purpose is

Our vision is

Our mission is

Our Values are

Our philosophy of ministry or service is

How does the current group of leaders' statements compare with the original statements like these when the church was planted or the institution was birthed?

These types of statements help to create strategy and structure allowing the team and people to run with the vision and communicate properly.

VISION ALIGNMENT

Another vital question must be asked and answered, when the above basic statements are in place. It falls under the vision statement and is vital to transition/succession planning.

The question is, *What do we want the community we serve to say about us twenty years from now?*

The answer to this question must be reduced to a simple statement. Ideally, this question should be answered by the head pastor or chief leader, middle managers or elders/deacons, and the successor, respectively, when possible.

This question can only be answered after assessing the needs of the community being served, the organization's resources, both financial and human, prayer and agreement. In other words, it doesn't just matter what you say in your vision and mission statements—you must find a niche in your community by listening and investigating. Then assess your resources and personnel. Applying kingdom culture and principles to needs like this will cause a church, business, nonprofit, or other entity to flourish and be blessed.

When the statement is determined, benchmarks are inserted into the plan to measure progress toward the stated goal. Now the organization has a direction, destination, and a way to measure progress.

When the principal leader, lead pastor, elders/deacons/successor/ sub-leadership are unified the next task becomes aligning the congregation/team and the ministries/departments of the organization with the vision.

We have observed many instances where staff personnel, leadership, and team members/congregants have differing views of vision destination and the process to get there. Chaos and disorder often result from the confusion.

In a church setting for example, the youth pastor, children's pastor, worship pastor, small group pastor, or a mission's pastor may have a conflicting viewpoint from the goals and destination articulated in the vision. Add the various interpretations of congregants, and the conflict magnifies. However minute the misalignment, over time and distance, misdirection creates organizational drag and momentum is lost. When momentum is lost, vision is rarely realized.

Occasionally, people join a church or organization for reasons other than forwarding the mission presented by the entity. Their objective is to draw attention to themselves and solicit support for their agenda. This creates counterproductive distraction, factions, and confusion. No organization is immune to this type of inner dissension. But proper alignment of the congregation/group and the ministries/departments, coupled with an accountability component, virtually eliminates this type of behavior.

Churches and nonprofits particularly cannot survive without volunteer assistance. However, it is lethal to empower unaligned people in serving positions.

Vision undermining by subordinates happens in business and for-profit entities. Far too many lead pastors and principals, are so busy with the "important stuff" they forget to be concerned with the vision clarity of the influencer two or three levels down. This leaves the organization susceptible to unrecognized dangers.

Unaligned people always create drag, inhibiting organizational momentum. On the other side of the spectrum are those aligned volunteers or staff leaders who clearly understand the vision, know their operational function, and are accountable for their performance. The church or organization that communicates clear vision, enjoys the honor, harmony and synergy of leaders, congregants, subordinates, departments, and ministries who think of themselves as a productive team.

In an aligned organization, everyone knows the lane God has called them to run in as they serve Him through their position. They also know where the boundaries of their influence in the total vision picture is. They focus on their part as if it is the most important part and stay out of other lanes. The focus is to exceed the benchmark in their lane.

They are part of a blended whole that adds to the momentum toward the twenty-year vision plan. They understand that their actions and attitudes will affect what the community will say about the organization in twenty years.

PERFORMANCE ASSESSMENT/COACHING

Performance assessments are vital to progress measurement. These assessments are the last thing a principal leader wants to do, yet it is one of the most important functions of influencing well.

Jesus taught several parables on the servant's responsibility to account to the owner for his/her performance with his vineyard. (Matthew 21:33-41 NLT) Reward is always there for the responsible steward. We see assessments as teaching/coaching opportunities performed by leadership. They can offer epiphanies and opportunities like the one this father had.

A BETTER APPROACH

The son of a dear friend was a basketball player in high school. He was serious about his game and his father often went to his practices to watch him. The father noticed that the coach appeared brutal with his team. If they didn't run a particular drill the way he expected, he would yell and make them run laps. Many of the players threw up as the result of running those laps. He was amazed that despite the coach's borderline abuse, all the players loved, respected, and obeyed him. This confounded the father. He felt the coach got much less resistance when rebuking his son on the basketball court, than he did as a father, when he corrected him.

The father finally approached his son and asked, "Why is it that when the coach yells and screams at you in front of the other players, you not only obey him, but have great respect for him? That's only a game. But when I correct you, much more gently, so you can succeed in life, you give me so much resistance?"

The boy's answer stunned the father. "I'm sorry, Dad. I guess I trust that Coach's criticism is to make me a better player because it has. Your approach to correction feels like abstract censoring or that you're just criticizing me."

The problem ceased that day. The father changed his approach and became a life coach to his son. When occasions arose to teach his son, he explained that if he would consider adjusting his attitude, posture, or viewpoint he would reap much greater rewards in life. He painted a picture of outcome based on choice.

Now the man's son is grown and has his own family. They both serve in a local church. Today, if you were to ask the father or son what their relationship is like, both would say they are best friends.

Assessments are wonderful opportunities to coach those God has gifted you to influence. It is your job to help them improve their service. If a leader goes through several assessments and cannot hit the benchmark for the person they are shepherding, perhaps that person is not gifted for that particular position. Work to find out what gives them joy in service, assure them of their value to you and the mission of your organization, and help them find the position on the team that makes them shine and furthers the greater good.

By doing so, you will have helped them avoid a potential burnout. You have positioned them in the place God gifted them for, and their greatest fulfillment is realized.

They will be forever grateful and so will you.

Clear vision and alignment of congregants and ministries, team members and departments, with an accountability component, allows the organization or church to gain and maintain momentum. Like the church in the Book of Acts, it positions a group of 21st century people to be in one place, in one accord, speaking the same thing, causing God to add to the church daily those that are to be saved. In community language, you can provide immediate benefit, but also offer the potential for eternal legacy impact. (Acts 2:1,47)

It was the famous CEO of General Electric, Jack Welch, who stated,

"Good business leaders create a vision, articulate the vision, passionately own the vision, and relentlessly drive it to completion."

If it is true for business, how much more important it is for us who lead God's people from one season to the next in a church or organizational setting. Especially and including transition. Like Joshua, who as a leader transitioned from Moses and wilderness wandering to city-taking and inheritance gaining, leaders are called and commissioned to ensure the continuum of God's purpose in the church and for their communities (Deuteronomy 34:1-5, Joshua 1:1-2).

ASK YOURSELF AND OTHERS . . .

- How do the leaders today see the organization's vision in comparison to its vision at its founding?

- If there are differences, what has brought about those differences?

- Where does alignment need to happen to bring about unity of vision?

- How often do leaders and subordinates need to discuss vision and realign to the core or original vision of the organization?

CHAPTER 6

The Prosperity of Financial Planning

"No person was ever honored for what he received. Honor has been the reward for what he gave."

—Calvin Coolidge

The Cost of Honor

Some senior leaders will turn to this chapter in the book first. The reason is, most of our clients start their exit strategy planning with the financial security arrangements in the forefront of their minds. This is understandable. It is also the area that can be the most problematic, and for a variety of reasons.

There are two predictable financial scenarios that leaders face when planning to step down.

1. A conventional retirement benefit has been pre-established for the leader provided through a formally structured business, non-profit, or denominational church setting. This chapter may not apply to them, although *they are not disqualified* from the need to examine supplemental means of retirement.

2. The individual who has not been provided for by a day-job, denomination, or board, after their service ends. This is our primary focus in this chapter.

The first, and most common reason a missing financial retirement package can be problematic, is that a founding leader has typically sunk all extra personal monies into the work or church they built. They have made sacrifices over the years for the work; and that leader, if he's not selfish or self-serving, has led the way in giving much up.

While other members might also sacrificially give to help build the work, many are taken care of in their retirement years by a plan established through other means. Sometimes, their main source of employment comes from a day-job providing retirement vehicles, funded over a long period of time. While others may benefit from contributions made to their spouse's retirement plan.

But for leaders and pastors who have invested their best work years into laboring for the organization or church, retirement can sneak up on them, leaving them unprepared. For a clear majority of churches and ministries in particular, this is one of the most overlooked and sensitive/touchy areas in transition and succession planning.

Why Retirement Planning for Senior Leader(s) Must Be Explored

There is:

*   a hesitation by the leader to even approach the subject with his board, cabinet, or oversight committee, for fear of appearing self-interested.

- a lack of knowledge on the part of the leader and his/her board or compliance group, concerning the process needed to fund and provide for a leader's future.

Too often, the church and many nonprofits, along with their leaders, have left this component out. Not only out of their succession preparation thinking, but out of their stewardship awareness and planning from day-one of the institution's inception and start.

Why? Because we all think we will be leading until Jesus comes!

There is a singular question the leadership must ask. "What is the honorable thing to do?"

The Bible tells us, when speaking of elders, *Let the elders who rule well, be counted worthy of double honor, especially those who labor in the word and doctrine.* (1 Timothy 5:17).

Eugene Petersen in The Message said this, regarding 1 Corinthians 9:8-12,

> *I'm not just sounding off because I'm irritated. This is all written in the scriptural law. Moses wrote, "Don't muzzle an ox to keep it from eating the grain when it's threshing." Do you think Moses' primary concern was the care of farm animals? Don't you think his concern extends to us? Of course. Farmers plow and thresh expecting something when the crop comes in. So if we have planted spiritual seed among you, is it out of line to expect a meal or two from you? Others demand plenty from you in these ways. Don't we who have never demanded deserve even more?*

That's rather blunt!

So, the question remains. "What is the honorable thing to do?"

This is the best time to show a confidence in God's provision and His assured blessing, by handling this sensitive area with transparency, honesty, faith and gratitude. However, too many leaders and boards will suddenly get stingy, exhibit smallness of thinking, and show a complete void of faith whenever finances and matters of financial planning are addressed.

The following compilation case-study is based on true stories of churches we have dealt with in our years of consulting. Please remember, this example can be told over and over with different cities, different organizations, and varying paradigms, but the end result always seems to remain the same: dishonor, disorder, confusion, ungratefulness, and faithlessness.

AN ATMOSPHERE OF HONOR REGARDING FINANCES

Check the qualities your organization or church exhibits toward finances

- Stingy
- Transparent
- Faithless
- Generous
- Grateful
- Honest
- Realistic Stewardship
- Honoring

THE FAILURE TO PLAN BRINGS FAILURE

Pastor Bill had founded and pastored the church for the last 25 years. The church was medium sized, but had a good reputation in the city, and a faithful congregation that enjoyed the blessings of God—mainly because of their integrity and the fidelity they maintained to their vision. They were not stingy and had given large sums to missions, both locally and internationally. They paid their staff appropriately and exhibited a balanced approach to faith and finances.

For some reason, the senior leader, sensing a new potential open door of ministry in another sphere of influence, unwisely got up during a Sunday morning service and announced, "Today will be my last sermon to you as pastor. I am turning over the church to a young man you all know in this congregation."

There was an audible gasp from the lips of everyone in the room, including the appointed young man. He had not been told of this decision, nor had the leadership board been brought into the decision. Other than the senior leader's spouse, everyone instantly felt confused, hurt and dumbfounded.

Shortly after the Sunday morning meeting, when it came time for the new leader and board to discuss what a good and honorable severance and retirement package looked like, the new leader strongly resisted the suggestion of the predecessor. The predecessor had high expectations, but the successor (and board) were so enraged at how everything had been handled, they determined to hardly offer any funds whatsoever. This caused the predecessor to attempt a re-do decision, hoping to reverse his plans of succession.

In the meantime, to make matters worse, the new open door of ministry he thought was available to him closed, and he found himself out of a job, out of a church, and out of money. The successor and the board finally and begrudgingly determined to give the predecessor a small percentage of what he had been accustomed to making. It most certainly wasn't sufficient, and the predecessor ended up taking a minimal pay full-time job.

Today, he has no place of honor in the "house" he had given his life to. He has no sense of financial security in his retirement, and he now endures the embarrassment of an unwise decision and the resentment of a successor who wants nothing to do with him.

In another case, a medium sized inner-city pioneer church was founded and had been pastored by the same man for over forty years. Approaching his mid-seventies, he now felt tired and weary, and knew it was beyond time to transition the church to a younger man. The senior pastor felt the church needed the energy and relevance necessary to take it into the next season.

Sad to say, no plans were in place for securing his financial security post-pastoring—nothing had even been discussed or initiated. The church could not afford a new, younger pastor with any monies left to bless and honor the founder and former leader. The difficult question required an answer.

Does the founder stay in the pulpit and in charge until he dies, or do you let him go to fend for himself and hope for the best?

Ultimately, the predecessor ended up leaving and lived his final days almost as poor as the poverty-stricken people he had helped for years. Social security and the odd jobs were all he had at the end, and the odd jobs soon became unavailable, as his age prohibited him from working.

This image paints a very real and difficult circumstance that so many great leaders find themselves in. Because of how they filed their taxes, some don't even have social security to rely on. This also creates a deeply challenging situation confronting the successor every time he cashes his paycheck. It's a no-win dilemma for all concerned—and does not represent the blessings God promises His people.

THE GREATEST STUMBLING BLOCKS

There are some very common stumbling blocks that every church and leadership team must recognize and determine to address. In no special order, they are:

- *Denial.* This relates to the leader who imagines himself never dying, remaining totally unstoppable, and relevant to all generations. Everyone loves to hear this individual speak.
- *Failure.* Usually, because of the above denial, the organization has resisted taking any steps to plan for the future. There is no preparation for the leader's future (post-governance), a successor's future, or the entity's future. Particularly in church scenarios, the exiting pastor has no life insurance, has opted out of social security, has no will, or no plan for sudden death sickness/disability.
- *A false understanding of true faith.* Faith without works (planning) is dead, we are told in the Word.[11] But occasionally, a person will insist they have faith, and great faith, and even super-faith about their future provision. But super faith or hyper faith, is nothing but fear in disguise—and it keeps too many from planning appropriately.
- *Waiting.* Lingering too long, to put a needed financial plan into place creates peril. Unexpected change, sickness, or even death can happen in a second and without warning, endangering the individual and/or organization.

---

11 https://www.biblegateway.com/passage/?search=James+2%3A14-26&version=NKJV

DETERMINE THE FINANCIAL NEEDS FOR THE PREDECESSOR AND SUCCESSOR

All situations and circumstances are different. If anyone comes along and tries to offer you some financial advice or planning that doesn't take into account your particular situation and entity structure, politely pay them little attention. The way an organization was started, the history, culture, resources, assets and liabilities should all be considered. Understand, typically all churches and every business started from nothing. Rarely, is anything begun with unlimited financial resources. Especially in nonprofit structures, there is often little or no thought given to retirement finances or funding for future generations.

Pastors are often desperate for advice and ideas on how to plan the next season in their lives. They are looking not only for some career direction and how to approach a new phase, post-pastoring, but how to plan and fund that new season comfortably and most certainly without creating a drain on the church they founded and served for so many faithful years.

Founding pastors in particular, want to continue to minister, but in a different venue—and there is a great need for these types of leaders beyond the church they initially served. Funding for the founding pastor must include assessing the pastors' role in the church, going forward.

Will he or she take a subordinate position?

Will he or she move on and generate other income?

Every situation is different. A church with 4000 people will be different from a church with 400 people. Hope is found by starting as early as possible. Even a ten-year period prior to eventual transition, would surprise most at how much can be done. Delay is never an option.

At the very least, communicate with someone outside the church who has both the experience and knowledge base to offer you some wise counsel and advice. Think of it as a simple algebra problem. Everyone (every church or organization) has TIME (T), and everyone (every church and organization) has MONIES (M), and everyone (church and organization) is looking for a certain RESULT (R).

If you can offer the equation at least an adequate amount of monies (M), then the more time (T) you can provide, the greater the results (R). However, if you have little T, then you're going to have to increase the contribution of M, in order to see certain R and meet some expectations.

In rare circumstances, there is very little T and hardly any M. This is where a qualified consultant must work with a board in a creative way to try and produce a sufficient R. It's hard—but not impossible.

Securing the Future and Funding the Next Generation

Not everyone is facing a crisis in this area. Many pastors we meet continue to minister; but the church planned in advance, so when the next lead pastor (successor) was ready, it wasn't a financial burden. This allowed the founder to be a source of strength and blessing to the local church and others beyond the church and organization. This same philosophy of honor and order allows for successful transitions in businesses and nonprofits.

We call this "funding the future." Without thinking about the right way regarding this, leaders or leadership teams could be inclined to resist talking about or planning for the future of the founding pastor or predecessor. If done correctly, and with enough advanced planning, the investments made today will actually have the effect of financing the future. This approach in planning will not only adequately cover and support the predecessor, but ultimately fund subsequent generations of leaders—allowing lasting impact to continue on.

THE CONGREGATION'S (TEAM) REWARD

We have found that congregations and teams, are funny things. People have interesting thoughts about all sorts of topics.

The one topic a leadership team never wants to face begins with the question, "How are you taking care of the person who's taken care of us all these years?"

Typically, if they see the pastor or leader suffering lack or poverty-stricken in retirement, or even facing sickness, they never come back to the pastor and rebuke him or her regarding indecision or lack of planning on that leader's part. They will, however, take a metaphorical baseball bat to the heads of the leadership team for not having "provided for their shepherd."

Ultimately, you don't want to face an angry group. You want to lead ahead of any conflict or unforeseen circumstance. Therefore, the best remedy is taking the time now to address the future as a leader concerned for your followers. Consult with your leadership team and get appropriate outside help, who will provide knowledge and expert input on the difficult subject of succession planning and retirement funding.

At the minimum, indicate to your leadership team how to respond, and who will temporarily take the authority role, should the unforeseen happen. Don't leave your leadership team and most certainly the people you shepherd, in the position of floundering without direction or guidance. At the very least, provide a temporary solution until a more complete permanent solution can be established.

Refuse to leave your people to the whims of a denomination, board, or other advisory group that really doesn't intimately know your culture.

Do not throw them into the swirling emotions of the moment without direction, because a shepherd is not there.

A congregation, employees, or volunteers find rest and comfort in the knowledge that they will be well taken care of—this is the reward they receive from orderly planning following a biblical honoring process. The leadership finds peace in knowing there is a plan in place that will be executed to insure the continuity of ministries and/or missions.

You only have to look at Jesus for such a perfect example. Not only was He the greatest disciple maker and teacher, but He was the ultimate shepherd and the perfect farsighted CEO. It was He who repeatedly prepared His followers for His departure. One day He said, (and I'm paraphrasing), "I am going soon (succession planning) to prepare a place for you . . . but don't be upset or afraid—I will send you a comforter (a designated replacement of me) and he will abide with you forever." (John 14:2-3)

Wow! He planned for the future of his church, considered the lives of his followers in that plan, comforted them by letting them know certain parts of the plan, and made sure he left them in good hands and in a peaceful state of mind. What a great leader—what an excellent CEO.

ASK YOURSELF AND OTHERS . . .

In the back of this book there is an appendix with FAQs, but we wanted to cover a few questions here at the end of this chapter, based on what we seem to always encounter:

1. *When should we start succession planning?*

    At least 10 years before transition is optimal (although sooner is always better). The least amount of time we recommend before transition is 4-5 years. You want an adequate and honorable severance or retirement package.

2. *We don't have a large amount to put in now—what do we do?*

    There are strategies and plans available that work well, if you start early enough.

3. *We're a small entity with very limited resources—what do we do?*

    - Early planning and consultation is key.
    - Get rid of your fears—face your limited parameters and let us help you find a plan that will work.

4. *How can I be sure I will be paid?*

    We have developed with our team of experts a way and means that insures these funds can never be subverted into something else or denied the beneficiary. These means are not only legal but also IRS approved for pastors and key leaders.

5. *Can the organization or church somehow benefit?*

    Yes! Our plans always come with a means to offer, in perpetuity, for both the predecessor and the subsequent successors. This needed funding has the potential to generate income downward into multiple succeeding generations and is designed to be a win-win for the organization along with current and future leaders.

6. *How can I begin this now?*

    Contact our team for a phone consultation and let us help you set things into motion.

REMEMBER — the sooner you start — the easier the plan will be, and the greatest results will be realized.

CHAPTER 7

THE PRAGMATICS OF THE PRACTICALS, TIMELINES, DOCUMENTS

"Order and simplification are the first steps towards mastery of a subject."

— Thomas Mann

M uch emphasis has been placed on honor in this book. We believe it is the catalyst for success throughout the transition/succession process. It is as important at this stage of the transition/succession journey as it is in any other part of the process. But to maintain honor, there must be order.

We refer to the information shared in this chapter as the "practicals" because it provides an overview of the documentation and timelines necessary for the entire transition/succession and focuses beyond. Leaders, more often than not, struggle when dealing with their own season of transition. An emotionally healthy influencer will want to plan his transition/succession path well. His/her focus is the success-ful "baton hand-off" to the successor in a manner that preserves the continuity of the entity's vision after succession. The wellbeing of the people, and their standing in the community, is a priority. Prayer is always a prerequisite.

Time spent reviewing, adjusting, and producing a written transition plan with documentation and timelines help to govern the pace, and measure transition progress—these are vital to success. When a well-constructed transition/succession plan is formulated, adapted, and followed, order rather than chaos guides the way. This brings honor to God and to the to the community of people being served—internally and externally.

WHOM DO I CALL FIRST?

If you as the leader are certain that this is your season of transition and your spouse has had adequate time to process the idea and is in complete agreement, who is the first person you should call?

It's no secret that most pastors, presidents, CEO's, or other persons in positions of authority, need the help of others to begin developing a transition/succession plan. Some seek advice of a friend outside the church or business. Others seek help from an older, well-respected retired pastor or former organizational head, who has been through one or more transition/succession experiences.

While thousands of baby boomers are retiring and millennials are taking their places, someone has to be called in to assist in trying to straighten out transition/successions gone bad, after attempts with little or no forethought. This is why we recommend your first call be made to a consulting company who can professionally guide you through the process, or to an experienced individual who has success-fully navigated a transition. But the second number you dial should be to the most trusted member of your board.

We are friends with a well-known pastor of a megachurch in the south whose father was the founding pastor. Our friend had been on the mission field for a time as a young man and had returned to the church after his tour of duty was over. He was sitting on the front row of the church on a Wednesday night when his father approached the pulpit to teach.

As the elder pastor began, he announced that his time was over and his son would be taking the lead role in the church—beginning right then. The son was as shocked as the congregation. Somehow, that church not only survived, but thrived and became one of the great churches in our country. We don't know of any other situation where such a spontaneous strategy has succeeded.

We do know that no plan is a plan—it is a plan to fail.

CONSTITUTION AND BY-LAWS WITH AMENDMENTS

The person presently seated in the highest position of authority is the ideal person to lead the preparation and process of transition/ succession. His/her work should start with reviewing the Constitution, By-Laws and Amendments to ensure that any transition/succession planning remains consistent with those documents. Often, amendments are added to the constitution to address transition protocol for future leadership changes.

If the entity has existed for many years, the Constitution and By-Laws may need to be updated, revised or amended to meet current state law, or to better reflect its values, approach, and how it governs itself in modern cultural and social shifts. This review should not only consider where the organization is at present, but the vision and mission plan for the future should also be considered to determine if adjustments are required. Professional legal advice is recommended for this endeavor.

SETTING DOWN AND STICKING TO A TRANSITION/ SUCCESSION PLAN AND TIMELINE

Every church and organization should have a transition/succession plan. Unfortunately, very few do. These plans can and should be on file years in advance, because they address the step-by-step process for the leadership to follow when the time for change arrives.

Unplanned transitions are common; and without a clear and orderly map to follow, the entity suffers the consequences. The vision becomes blurred, momentum is lost, forward process ceases, honor is aborted and confusion reigns. Unplanned transitions are often triggered by circumstances such as: the unexpected death of the lead pastor, sexual immorality, theological shifts, money misappropriation, etc. If your organization does not have a leadership contingency plan in place, you would do well to see that one is put in place ASAP, before all is lost.

Planning however, remains only a concept unless a timeline is superimposed on it. A timeline is also useless unless action is taken to bring the transition/succession plan to fruition. Accomplishment breeds confidence and movement, which produces momentum. We recommend transition consultation three to five years out, and fifteen to twenty years out, if the succession includes creating a retirement package for the outgoing leader.

It is imperative that the timeline allows an adequate allotment for each phase of the plan to be done well. Once the timeline is established for each phase of the process, you will be able to see the approximate time for the entire transition to be achieved. Leadership, oversight, management and accountability for each task delegated, are musts to keep the transition on pace for a successful and timely outcome. Sometimes, the process moves more quickly than anticipated, and there will be times when it appears that the bottom has fallen out and there is no forward movement. Expect the feelings but ground yourself by referring to your plan and projected timeline.

These scenarios beg the question, *When can I be flexible and when am I to be rigid?*

We think flexibility is always in order, unless there are issues with focus and performance, preventing forward movement. Also, flexibility is in order when legal documentation through a law firm, an insurance provider, etc. is held up and there is nothing that can be done while you wait on others to finish their part.

We believe regular transition team meetings that include reporting and team accountability, as well as coaching and encouraging, are vitally important. The end-goal must always be presented, and progress reported, delays explained, and the way forward clearly presented. Firmness is appropriate in the exercise of these functions because they create and maintain a winning spirit and momentum on the team.

COVERING ALL THE LEGAL BASES IN YOUR TRANSITION

One of the things we do through Seira Group, is to retain a law firm to prepare all the legal documentation required through the transition/succession process for our clients. We take the worry out of it. If, however, you are attempting a do-it-yourself approach to legal documentation, we highly recommend that you retain legal help for review. Constitution, By-laws, Constitutional Amendments, Financial Documentation, Retirement Contracts, Trust funds, etc. fall into legal document categories that need professional legal attention.

ASK YOURSELF AND OTHERS . . .

- Who is putting together the formal transition plan and timeline?

- Who is advising/consulting with the lead authority and organizational leadership on the transition?

- What legal bases are essential to cover now?

"Although some organizations today may survive and prosper because they have intuitive geniuses managing them, most are not so fortunate. Most organizations can benefit from strategic management, which is based upon integrating intuition and analysis in decision making. Choosing an intuitive or analytic approach to decision making is not an either–or proposition. Managers at all levels in an organization inject their intuition and judgment into strategic-management analyses. Analytical thinking and intuitive thinking complement each other.

"Operating from the I've-already-made-up-my-mind-don't-bother-me-with-the-facts mode is not management by intuition; it is management by ignorance. Drucker says, "I believe in intuition only if you discipline it. 'Hunch' artists, who make a diagnosis but don't check it out with the facts, are the ones in medicine who kill people, and in management kill businesses."

— Fred R. David, *Strategic Management:
Concepts and Cases, Instructor Review Copy*

CHAPTER 8

THE PROCESS OF MONITORING AND EVALUATING THE SUCCESSION PLAN

"Fear cannot be banished, but it can be calm and without panic; it can be mitigated by reason and evaluation."

— Vannevar Bush

Each chapter of this book offers information and insight that any church, nonprofit, ministry, or business would be well served to include in its transition/succession planning. If your organization does not currently have such a plan, the insights offered here may serve to guide you in developing one that fits your context. The safety and security provided by a transition design is not restricted to long-term planning for a meticulous, seamless succession on a set day in the distant future. It can also be an entity-saver in different scenarios and other circumstances.

A good succession plan may provide the shining light that guides the organization through the darkness and confusion when the unexpected happens. The loss of a lead authority figure through extended sickness, an untimely death, immorality, divorce or scandal, happens more often than not.

Once transition/succession is initiated, the design guides the process. Monitoring and evaluating each phase of the succession plan, however, becomes paramount. There are too many moving parts in the transition process to think that the desired result can be realized without oversight. Scheduling, delegation, task assignments, benchmarks, accountability, assessment, coaching the team when the eventual, unexpected delays and pitfalls occur, keep the process on track.

No plan, however good and personalized to context, produces results on its own, any more than a building blueprint creates a building. Activating the plan, monitoring the execution of the plan and evaluating the progress of each facet at every stage of the plan are critical to a positive outcome.

Interestingly, when the plan works, the team gets the honor. If the transition process falters or fails, the blame is usually ascribed to the design. A successful succession results from working the plan. An asset of incalculable value is having competent team members who take ownership of their assigned tasks and make themselves accountable to the senior leader for their performance. Maintaining focus on doing quality work, hitting benchmarks, meeting timelines, maintaining positive attitudes, encouraging team spirit, with lots of communication flow, etc. are all parts of a winning combination.

Honest Honor

"Real transformation requires real honesty. If you want to move forward, get real with yourself first." –Bryant McGill

Each chapter of this book stresses the importance of honorable design and order in a transition. Monitoring and evaluating the succession planning process is no different—and honest honor must be established and maintained even in the practical matters of leadership change.

There really isn't a pastor/leader who hasn't been guilty at some point of using "evangelistic-speech" on just about every subject pertaining to the health and progress of the church, non-profit, or business he or she leads. Some will slightly (more in the case of some leaders) inflate attendance or financial numbers, or expound beyond reality, their vision and progress in community reach. Sometimes you can get away with exaggerations of this sort, but usually only for short periods of time.

Honesty is critically needed in the measuring and gauging of readiness and execution of a planned exit or transition strategy. This is where you don't want to get things wrong, nor set into motion a plan, that when played out, is found so wanting in detail, failure is almost assured. Too many lives are affected when dishonesty taints the picture, but worse, the reputation of the organization or its work within the larger community can suffer an almost overnight collapse of its reputation and strong history. Self-honesty leads to significant change.

EXECUTING THE SUCCESSION PLANNING PROCESS REQUIRES
- Diligent leadership marked by honest honor and humility.
- Intergenerational teamwork.
- Openness to change.
- Positive, effective communication.
- Accountability.
- Monitoring and Evaluation.

There comes a time in every church or organization where significant change is required. Aging leaders, maintaining generational relevance, a weariness in the journey, or a false preservation of authority or position are all components in any organization that needs a periodic honesty assessment. And it's the senior leader that must initiate this assessment.

We have met many leaders who refuse to be honest with themselves when it becomes obvious to others that change is required. For example, if you're eighty years old and still the senior leader of your church, chances are, you are living in a dream. Thinking you're knocking it out of the park with twenty-year-old adults is likely self-deluding.

Another area lacking honesty comes from grasping at and an unwillingness to let go of, the authority, esteem, and position held for so many years and decades. This must be dealt with in the emotional intelligence assessment; but nonetheless an honest evaluation must also be made of why change is resisted. The leadership of an organization exhibiting honest honor at every level can end up being dishonest and showing no honor, when they react with fear to making the necessary evaluations and changes.

To create and maintain a culture of honor, we must extend honest honor into the area of our own self-assessment, then extend it to the organization as well. You honor the Lord and the ones you lead when you do this, you also honor yourself. This honest honor should continue during the transition plan execution and for many years following. The by-product of honest honor is, in fact, honor itself.

WHAT IS EVALUATION?

"One of the great mistakes is to judge policies and programs by their intentions rather than their results." –Milton Friedman

Webster defines evaluate as:

1. to determine or fix the value of,
2. to determine the significance, worth, or condition of, usually by careful appraisal and study.

Evaluation is the accountability and quality control measures used by the overseer (usually lead pastor, president, CEO, etc.) to calculate actual progress toward each benchmark of the transition/succession design. Proper evaluation also serves to bring a sense of sobriety to the planning process. How one views transition/succession preparedness determines the value they place upon it. The value we place on something determines the time and effort we are willing to relegate to it. This is not simply our hypothesis—this truth is documented as far back as the Bible.

Judas sold out Jesus for thirty pieces of silver, while Paul said, "Yes, everything else is worthless when compared with the infinite value of knowing Christ Jesus my Lord. For his sake, I have discarded everything else, counting it all as garbage, so that I could gain Christ and become one with him." (Matthew 26:14-16; Philippians 3:8)

Obviously, Paul was seeing something in Jesus that Judas missed! Proper evaluation helps people see the value of a person or thing, including the importance of planning for generational transition.

We have encountered several instances where pastors have announced from the pulpit, "This is my last sermon as the lead pastor of this church." This happened without informing anyone that such an announcement was eminent.

This sort of behavior begs the question, *"Why would anyone do such a thing?"*

A leader often spends his/her career loving, caring, serving their congregation, team, and community. They cast vision and organize and equip the organization to accomplish its mission. They provide shepherding care, encouragement and guidance. Pastors in particular, are purveyors of hope. How then, does a professional rationalize that somehow a sudden announcement, without providing the safety and security of a well-written design, including a commitment to oversee and guide that plan, is somehow the right thing to do?

Why would a pastor/leader dishonor his entire body of work, his legacy and future, by leaving his people who have loyally walked with him and a successor (named or unnamed) to clean up the mess, because of one ill-advised moment of discouragement, fatigue, or poor planning?

WHO DOES THE EVALUATING?

Transition/succession must be viewed as a process, not an event. As such, a solid design must include the end goal as well as each step necessary to reach it. Much value and honor are added to the entity that prioritizes the creation of a well-constructed transition/succession plan and carries it out to completion.

The person in the highest position of authority should direct the board/leadership team/elders/deacons through the process of producing an honorable transition design, except in cases of a sudden and unexpected circumstance that involves the absence of that leader. The plan should be put in writing and produced (if possible) far in advance of an actual transition/succession.

Most organizations do not have such a document and especially suffer when an unexpected moral failure, illness, untimely death of the leader, etc., forces them into transition/succession. We wrote this book and founded our company to assist you in creating this crucial agreement.

CRUCIAL KEYS TO SUSTAINING SUCCESSION EFFORTS

Sustaining support depends upon several factors.

- The quality and clarity of the transition plan, and properly communicating it, is imperative.

- Unity of the leadership with everyone speaking the same dialogue concerning the transition/succession design is vital to getting buy-in and support of the plan from the people.
- Consistent, clear communication, with updates on progress through each phase of the transition/succession plan helps to build and maintain momentum. Open communication keeps the team aware and engaged throughout the process.
- Reaching each benchmark within the allotted time frame creates excitement, fosters confidence and builds momentum.
- A positive leadership attitude sustains support for the succession effort. Support from the people requires the entire leadership team to project unity, confidence, stability and excitement about what God is doing, and a sense of His favor upon the plan and the entire organization.

MID-COURSE CORRECTIONS AND OTHER PITFALLS

We recommend a transition/succession model that allows for unexpected circumstances and other pitfalls. However, no design is perfect. Planning to complete each phase of the outline well, is more important than a fixed transition/succession date that has left key elements of the plan unfinished. When issues arise that warrant more time to resolve, include pertinent information to those that need to know and will be affected. Don't be afraid to communicate the need for more time to resolve the issue before moving on.

Board members, senior leaders, management, elders, deacons, team members and congregants appreciate having current knowledge. No one likes to be blindsided by a question they can't answer, due to lack of communication, especially in an area they have some responsibility. Expect some potholes in the journey and work hard to keep the transition/succession road open for traffic, even when repairs are in progress.

THE ROLE OF COACHING

In every organization we have worked with, we have found an amazing similarity. You can predict the existence of people who will jump on the transition/succession train right away, others who are not for or against it, and those who will outright fight it. Does this resonate with you?

This is why God chose you to help guide this important endeavor. The best approach is to thank God for all who catch the vision quickly and turn attention to those who will add their support at some point. You may not succeed in convincing them all, but you can get most of them on board. Even the transition/succession team members are going to need some help along the journey.

There are thousands of gravestones in the transition/succession planning graveyard. This is primarily due to the highest leader waxing authoritarian when people fail to meet the expected benchmarks, or question the pace, timelines, decision-making, etc. along the succession journey. Leaders should adopt a coaching style that constructively adjusts the team when issues arise and encourages them regularly in their tasks.

The military operates on an authority structure that says, "Salute the rank, even if you don't respect the man or woman wearing the uniform." Authoritarians order participation in a mission regardless of the feelings of the person being ordered to accomplish it. But the average person may not understand the mission they have been assigned. In war, this posture may work, but the transition/succession model must be viewed differently.

A leader/coach realizes that each person on the team is valuable to the team effort. Coaching includes helping the team members in:

- understanding the task
- knowing each person's role on the team

- being aware of their individual and team potential and calling them to step up to realize it
- encouraging, assessing, and adjusting each member's individual performance to help them reach their full potential
- remembering that there are personal and corporate rewards associated with their success

If a person falters in an assignment or task, instead of a rebuke, the coach steps in. Neither the team member's value or importance to the team is at stake—therefore, they view adjustment in a positive way. The team member knows the process serves to help them succeed. The authority figure must have a servant leader attitude, "Let him/her who would be the greatest, become the servant of all." (Mark 9:35)

Your last body of work as the leader should reflect on you as loving guide who gently, patiently, affectionately, but firmly, leads the organization through the transition/succession planning process into lush green pastures of promise and security in the future. You can do it!

"A coach is someone who can give correction without causing resentment."

—John Wooden

ASK YOURSELF AND OTHERS . . .

- Who is coaching and mentoring the transition process?

- What are the most important qualities this coach must possess?

- What are the greatest challenges this person will face?

"Momentum builds success."

—Suzy Kassem, *Rise Up and Salute the Sun:
The Writings of Suzy Kassem*

CHAPTER 9

THE PRESENCE OF SPIRITED MOMENTUM

"Momentum is the bridge between vision and its success."
— Farshad Asi, *How Important is Honor?*

n each of the preceding chapters, emphasis has been placed on the importance of honor and order as the bedrock of every phase of the transition/succession experience. Order with honor must become the undergirding prerequisite for the entire transition experience. When order with honor is the guiding principle, the transition/succession design is built in a respectful, emotionally mature manner, producing confidence in leadership at every stage.

Honor and order foster feelings of security, identity and a sense of belonging among people. Competing negative forces; such as, back-biting, gossip, division, striving and competition, are harnessed and restricted by honor and order. As honor is strengthened, momentum increases. Add order and momentum soars. Everyone wins and a testimony that glorifies God is presented in the community.

WHAT IS MOMENTUM?

One definition of momentum is, "the force or speed of movement; impetus, as of a physical object or course of events,"

Think of soap box derbies and how the children in their speedsters gain momentum racing down a hill as a good example of momentum. Or, the opposite, a football team that repeatedly fails to convert on third down and loses their momentum.

In this chapter, we refer to momentum as the force or speed of movement a church or organization gains or loses in the transition/ succession planning process. Leadership and the people they serve are most vulnerable to losing momentum, hope, and enthusiasm, during times of lead authority change. Most people may not understand or recognize the dynamics of momentum and its effect on forward movement; however, when momentum is lost, everyone knows something very important is missing.

Careful planning, emotional maturity, patience, vision, proper communication, prayer and incremental execution of a well-prepared plan help to consolidate the support and energy of leaders and congregants. This in turn produces enthusiasm that becomes the synergy and force fueling the necessary momentum vital to transition.

John Maxwell coach, Farshad Asi, remarks, "It takes a leader to create the momentum, it takes a vision to direct the momentum, it takes a massive action to build on the momentum, and it takes self-discipline to sustain the momentum. Momentum is the bridge between a vision and its results."[12]

In Acts 9:22 (MSG), we read, *But their suspicions didn't slow Saul [Paul] down for even a minute. His momentum was up now and he plowed straight into the opposition, disarming the Damascus Jews and trying to show them that this Jesus was the Messiah.*

The persecutor of the Jews, Saul, had met the risen Christ on the Damascus road. His newfound faith spurred him on and strengthened

---

12 https://www.goodreads.com/quotes/tag/momentum

him. To be strengthened, ἐνισχύω, is what Eugene Peterson chose to translate as momentum. In looking at the root meaning of *endunamoo*, it means "to be empowered."

Honor within an organization or church, and particularly between the most influential leader or lead pastor and his/her successor, empowers the entire group to communicate, plan, and execute transition effectively, increasing momentum toward a successful transition.

THE LEADER AND MOMENTUM—IT TAKES A LEADER TO CREATE MOMENTUM

A leader considering transition should view his transition as a relay race. He will be transferring the baton to another runner (his successor), who hopefully will bring home the gold medal. The proper handoff of the baton is critical. If dropped, the race is over. Timing and execution are paramount to a successful transfer of the baton.

MOMENTUM

- is the bridge between a vision and its results
- helps to power success
- arises from effective, servant leaders
- increases when personal agendas are set aside for what God wants and others need
- envisions the future and honors the past
- gains traction through self-discipline

Both the transitioning leader and his/her successor are on the same team. If the transitioning influencer has run their lap of the race with excellence and successfully handed off the baton, then the successor's chance of bringing home the gold medal significantly improves.

The better the outgoing leader and their team prepares for a successful transition, the more likely everyone understands and buys into the changes that take place throughout the transition journey.

Every consideration in the preceding chapters, if adopted and followed, come together to create a sense of honor, order, patience, cooperation, agreement, and responsibility. The people sense the favor of God is upon them. But this environment did not just mystically appear.

Honorable design and the art of orderly generational transition was created by the carefully planned, prayer-saturated efforts of the transitioning leader and his team. The plan, well communicated and executed, has created the force or speed of movement that we call momentum.

VISION DIRECTS MOMENTUM

The late Dr. Edwin Louis Cole, often said, "It is harder to maintain than to obtain."

Momentum is not easily gained but it is easily lost. Suzy Kassem commented, "When you find yourself in the thickness of pursuing a goal or dream, stop only to rest. Momentum builds success."

A must in the transition/succession design is vision, because it directs momentum. Just as highways direct traffic, vision directs momentum.

Not only does vision have a clear target or destination, it informs us of each waypoint on the journey to our destination. The clearer the vision the easier it is to maintain the momentum gained. The incremental preset benchmarks or waypoints in our vision plan inform us of our progress along the way. As each benchmark is checked off, joy and confidence build, which in turn increases our force or speed of movement.

Transition/succession planning snowballs through the incremental stages of the process. Starting with the highest authority figure, enthusiasm should grow as each layer of leadership, team, and person are communicated with about the details of the design. A very wise man, a long time ago said, "Without vision, the people perish." (Proverbs 29:18)

CONFIDENCE INCREASES MOMENTUM

Self-confidence and trust in the leadership, transition design, and the successor, fuels momentum. This ensures the chain of influence is strengthened and not easily broken. But some need to boost confidence as they face succession.

At times, many leaders feel insecure for many reasons discussed earlier in this book. When a CEO, president, senior manager, lead pastor, etc. takes the steps supporting honorable design for generational transition, confidence grows, and momentum is produced in the following ways:

- Raises your expectations and produces internal dissatisfaction.
- Dissatisfaction inspires motivation.
- Motivation energizes you to act.
- Action produces results.
- Results increase your confidence because you start to feel in control.
- Confidence grows.
- Momentum is produced.[13]

If a leader's confidence in themselves, or the transition plan, or the successor falters, momentum will decrease. The same is true if the successor's confidence fails.

---

13 Johnson, Keith *The Confidence Solution* New York, NY: Jeremy P. Tarcher Publishing 2011, p.9
115

To maintain and increase momentum, the leader must continually raise his/her expectation to . . .

- Place confidence in the Lord.
- Put confidence in the process and their successor.
- Produce actions that move the plans for transition forward.
- Pray with the leadership team for God to instill more confidence and to empower every positive step in the plan.

Remember that momentum (forward movement) will create issues, problems, and difficulties. Don't ignore or fear problems in the process.

Colin Powell said, "Leadership is solving problems. The day soldiers [or people in the organization in this case] stop bringing you their problems is the day you have stopped leading them. They have either lost confidence that you can help or concluded you do not care."[14]

Address each issue that arises with confidence and work on solving the problems as they arise, to maintain momentum toward your transition goals. This will lead to the outcome you desire.

IT TAKES MASSIVE ACTION TO BUILD ON MOMENTUM

Massive action is needed to build on momentum. Refuse to be passive or to procrastinate. Remember the massive Saturn V rockets NASA used to launch our astronauts into outer space?

Those rockets had three expendable stages. The first two each had five engines that burned either a mix of kerosene and liquid oxygen or liquid hydrogen and liquid oxygen. Each stage lifted the rocket until its fuel was expended. The first stage lifted the rocket about forty-two

---

14 https://www.brainyquote.com/topics/confidence

miles. The second carried it almost into orbit. The third stage placed the Apollo spacecraft into orbit and pushed it toward the moon. The products of the first two stages fell into the ocean after separation. The third stage either stayed in space or hit the moon.

Each was built on what the preceding stage had accomplished. As the rocket ascended and each stage was jettisoned, the rocket became much lighter and it took less force to maintain its momentum.

Each chapter in this book addresses a challenge that Seira Group consultants repeatedly encounter in churches and organizations facing the transition/succession planning process. It is our sincere desire that each of the chapters you read will move you closer to where you want to go, like the stages of the Saturn V. We hope to assist you in not only gaining momentum through the entire transition process, but to propel you successfully toward the conclusion of your vision, up to twenty years out and beyond.

IT TAKES SELF-DISCIPLINE TO SUSTAIN MOMENTUM

Self-discipline is required to develop and sustain momentum toward your goal.

Lori Myers describes it this way, "The Big push means it is the process of actively replacing excuses with winning habits, the ultimate excuses blockers. Moreover, it is being willing to go to the wall for what you want or believe in, to push beyond your previous mental and physical limits, no matter what it takes."

The apostle Paul, writing to the church at Corinth said, *Don't you realize that in a race everyone runs, but only one person gets the prize? So, run to win! All athletes are disciplined in their training. They do it to win a prize that will fade away, but we do it for an eternal prize. So, I run with purpose in every step. I am not just shadowboxing. I discipline my body like an athlete, training it to do what it should. Otherwise, I fear that after preaching to others I myself might be disqualified.* (1 Corinthians 9:24-27 NLT)

Some years ago, during a ministry visit to a church in Germany, we toured a very old cathedral. A brochure in the church described how the congregation, some 1100 years prior, had the foresight and faith to plant an oak tree forest the same time they laid the foundation of the cathedral. Some 400 years later, their descendants, using the oak wood from that forest, put on the roof. Now that's a vision plan! Can you imagine the task of carrying momentum forward 400 years and then building on it?

The importance of momentum cannot be overstated. Without it, the church and any organization, becomes stationary: stuck in time, stagnant, and irrelevant. Our goal must be to do our part to create and sustain an environment of momentum and build on it with each successive generation, until the return of our Savior Jesus Christ. He will someday appear to receive his glorious bride (the church) without spot, wrinkle, blemish, or any such thing. Your work makes a difference—now and into eternity. Your unbroken chain will support and save lives.

CHAPTER 10

A FINAL STEP

"It is through an unbroken chain of witnesses that we come to see the face of Jesus."

—Pope Francis

As the story goes, in 44 BC Gaius Julius Caesar bled to death from twenty-three stab wounds. In his will, Caesar had adopted and named as his successor, his grandnephew, Octavian. Only eighteen at the time, Octavian first appeared to be a marginal player compared to Marc Antony & Cleopatra (the mother of Caesar's biological son) and of little threat to Caesar's enemies. Octavian, however, proved a shrewd student.

Step by step over the course of two decades, Octavian transformed himself into the first emperor of Rome, known to history as Augustus. He ruled the empire for more than four decades. Augustus proved to be one of the most effective statesmen in history. He unified Rome, eliminating the civil wars that had ripped apart the Republic. He redesigned the system of government, brought peace, expanded the empire, and increased prosperity. He lived in a modest house and displayed a particular genius for political maneuvering, achieving objectives largely by making 'suggestions' rather than invoking formal legal or military power.

But Augustus failed to solve a chronic problem that significantly hurt the Empire over subsequent centuries—SUCCESSION!

After Augustus, Rome ping-ponged between competent leaders and semi-deranged titans like Caligula and Nero. The city never fully recovered, and the chain of effective leadership was broken.

Sad to say, too many church leaders and principals of non-profits and businesses have failed to plan for unforeseen eventuality. Any challenge, tragedy, or simply a new season in the organization can require a fresh leader—in other words—transition.

Reading this book should motivate you to take a preventative course of action by deciding to create your own transition plan, designed with honor and order. If you're a senior leader, it's critical you think this way, even if no one else on your team is discussing the topic. This means demonstrating your willingness to broach the subject with honesty and transparency. Find a means to educate yourself, as well as fostering knowledge among the men and women who serve with you in your organization. If you are a team member, consider approaching your pastor, senior leader, or other team members to offer this subject as an agenda item at your next meeting. Whatever your position, commit to helping keep your chain of leadership strong.

Peter Drucker, the great business guru said, "The ingredient most missing in churches today is a plan of succession. Ministers are getting older and the church is not thinking about the next generation." His statement is applicable for any organized group or business.

Those leaders who think beyond today and plan for the future, whether that be in financial planning, leadership pipe-line development, vision and values conversations, or momentum evaluations, represent those organizations who will see all they have done in their lifetime last for another generation and even beyond!

PROSPERING AFTER DEATH

Charles Spurgeon the great "prince of preachers" and pastor of Metropolitan Tabernacle in London for thirty-eight years, said this of his own church and its future. "I sometimes think if I were in heaven I should almost wish to visit my work at the Tabernacle, to see whether it will abide the test of time and prosper when I am gone. Will you hold to the grand old doctrines of the gospel? Or will this church, like so many others, go astray from the simplicity of its faith, and set up gaudy services and false doctrine? Methinks I should turn over in my grave if such a thing could be."

By 1908 (seventeen years after Spurgeon's death) almost everything that defined the church under Spurgeon had vanished. Spurgeon reached millions through his sermons, both spoken and published. But he did not train willing leaders capable of carrying on in his absence. Sadly, his chain of influence was weakened.

Cleanup crews sifting through the bombing rubble in 1941 discovered the church's 1680 confession of faith, which Spurgeon had symbolically buried beneath the foundation in 1860. Found in this recovery is a metaphor for the state of Spurgeon's church and the evangelical movement in England. There was in 1941 no influential congregation in England known to stand for the theology which that document contained, nor was there any college preparing men to preach that faith. By missing the creation of an honorable design, outlining the order of generational transition, Spurgeon severely impeded the ongoing power of the church he so passionately served.

WALKING OUT TRANSITIONAL CHANGE

In this short book, we have overviewed the most basic elements of succession planning and transition that should be taken into consideration. We recognize there are many more secondary issues that can be addressed as the need arises in any given organization's strategic planning. We also recognize that there are many influencers who do not like to think too much about future retirement, post-leadership, or even a second career in later years. To do so, to them, would feel almost a betrayal to the current call and position they hold.

But as three former long-term pastors, who each founded and led their local congregations for twenty-five plus years; and after having successfully navigated our own transitions and exits, we seek to offer our insight and experiences to help other leaders create an unbroken chain of influence. Succession planning is a hot topic these days, and many are talking and writing about it. The uniqueness of this book is that it is written by three pastors who have actually walked out transitional change to a victorious conclusion. You can read our personal stories at the end.

We want you to gain an edge when it comes to the difficult task of exit planning and strategy, so you achieve an unbroken chain of leadership influence. We are available to serve you and your congregation in transition, and invite you to contact us at:

Seira Group, LLC.

seiragroupllc@gmail.com

or visit our website at

seiragroup.org

Appendix

Succession Planning and Transition

FAQs

WHAT IS SUCCESSION PLANNING?

Wikipedia states it this way: Succession planning is a process for identifying and developing new leaders who can replace old leaders when they leave, retire or die. Too often however, many church pastors and leaders only address this topic when they are getting ready to step down. Wrong! Think of transition preparation as always keeping the leadership pipeline full to avoid interruption to the vision or mission of the organization. Remember, you don't know when you might leave this world or get sick and become incapacitated. That's not fear, that's fact, and it's also good planning and proper stewardship of what we've been entrusted with.

HOW IS SUCCESSION PLANNING DIFFERENT FROM REPLACEMENT PLANNING?

Ask any pastor or senior leader of a successful church/organization to define succession planning. There is a strong possibility that, if you do, you will find the average leader confuses replacement planning and succession planning. But they are truly not the same.

Replacement planning assumes that the organizational chart will remain unchanged over time. It usually identifies "backups" for top-level positions, as they are identified on the organizational chart, and stops there. A typical "replacement chart" will list about three people as "backups" for each top-level position and will usually indicate how ready each person is to assume the role of the current job incumbent. This certainly can be applied to that of a senior leader role. We view this as merely filling a job position (i.e., CEO, president, manager, senior pastor, pulpit-filler, etc.).

Succession planning, in contrast, specifically focuses on developing people rather than merely naming them as replacements. Its goal is to build deep bench strength throughout the organization so that, whenever a vacancy does occur, there is at least one person qualified (usually internally) that may be considered for advancement.

Additionally, succession planning deals strongly with the orderly processes required to ensure a smooth and successful transition between one leader and the next—and between one generation and the next. That is what we have attempted to address in this book. It is deliberate, intentional, and planned. Good leaders will recognize that it is wiser to focus beyond replacement planning to succession planning to build the long-term sustainability and viability of the church or organization. In the case of a church, hopefully, it was not founded only to become a one-generation wonder!

WHY IS SUCCESSION PLANNING NEEDED?

In the context of churches and other non-profit (ministry-focused) organizations, we have found there is a serious lack of succession planning at any level. For whatever reason, most senior leaders of churches or ministries tend to go out of their way to avoid approaching this subject within their own thinking or bringing the topic before their leadership team. We do recognize the all too real fear, that such thinking or discussion might create the appearance of dissatisfaction in the current role or indicate to others an attitude of flakiness and commitment to a long-term vision. And for some reason, a good business CEO receives kudos for his or her long-term and forward-thinking concerning succession planning, but in the church, it's considered either "faithless" or too "unholy."

The argument against this thinking is found in statistics that are all too real. Most churches when faced with succession/transition needs, find themselves so far behind the curve in planning, wisdom and execution, that failure is almost guaranteed. In fact, seven out of ten churches experiencing transition have stated that theirs was a failure (even if the church is still in existence) because of their failure to plan and take into account all the potential facets and emotions associated with a succession.

WHAT ARE THE ESSENTIAL COMPONENTS OF A SUCCESSFUL SUCCESSION PLAN?

Most consultant groups when asked this question will offer the following five key elements to successful succession planning. We list them here, but then have expounded on them to make them more applicable to the church/non-profit ministry context.

Identify the key position(s) for which a succession plan is necessary. The church may have (depending on the size) a couple of key positions that need to be taken into consideration. The senior leader/pastor is definitely one to be included in the succession plan. Some further considerations are:

- Is this a key role critical to the success of the organization, and if the person in this role suddenly leaves or is unavailable and the position becomes vacant, is the church or ministry at risk?

- Does the person currently occupying this position hold a good deal of knowledge about processes or other institutional memory that will effectively leave when the incumbent departs?

Identify the successor or successors. The church or ministry may not be ready to name a successor, but careful thought and consideration should be used here. Remember, you're not just filling a job. You are hopefully transitioning to another spiritual leader role, as an individual with a shepherd's heart, along with the necessary skill, knowledge, and emotional maturity to handle the difficult task of pastoring or leading a ministry. You need to make sure they fully understand the vision, mission, value, culture and philosophy of ministry that is currently present. Your goal is to ensure your successor is qualified for the position from day one and that the congregation or rest of the ministry sense and feel no discernable interruption of the flow of ministry.

Identify job requirements. Hopefully an identified successor will have been a part of the ministry or church long enough to understand what the job requirements are. However, we have seen successors brought into place; and after a year or so, look to make a change, because they (or more importantly their spouse) were blindsided by the great responsibility they have taken on. They were not prepared in advance for the price that would have to be paid. Prior to any succession announcement of personnel, it is wise, as an incumbent or predecessor, to make an inventory of skills, emotions, values and attributes that will serve as a checklist to audit what a succession candidate and his/her spouse presently offers and needs to develop.

Building competencies. The succession planning process must look at building the competencies and skills for current and future organizational needs. This is different than what was identified in the above requirement. Here, it is helping to answer the question, "What is next?" and not just "Who is next?"

There will be one set of competencies (i.e., skills, knowledge, abilities, emotional maturity) for each position. In designing a development plan to guide succession candidates into their intended future role and to strengthen their competencies, consider how a designated successor will take the church or ministry to even new heights and through new challenging seasons that will produce kingdom results. Increase, influence, impact, and inspiration should all see an up-swing under the successor's leadership. Real goals and targets should be set prior to the actual transition.

Assessing progress. As the father of modern management, Peter F. Drucker, correctly observed "What gets measured gets done."

It is essential that the organization, church, or ministry creates a succession plan and invests in the development of successors, as well as assesses its progress toward the intended outcome. Questions to be asked and metrics to be measured are as follows:

- Is a culture of honor established and being maintained even past the transition point?
- Are the core-values being honored even while the methodologies are changing?
- Has a clear order been established and communicated to all who will be affected?
- Are the church or ministries connecting well internally as well as externally into the community?
- Does the current succession plan support an unbroken chain of effective leadership?

WHAT ARE THE BIGGEST BENEFITS THAT AN ORGANIZATION OR CHURCH CAN EXPERIENCE FROM A SUCCESSION PLAN?

The death of iconic Apple CEO, Steve Jobs, highlights the benefits of establishing a proactive, not reactive, approach to succession planning. As his cancer progressed, Jobs knew his time as leader of the dynamic and innovative company would be ending. He wrote this in a resignation letter: "As far as my successor goes, I strongly recommend that we execute our succession plan and name Tim Cook as CEO of Apple."

By naming his successor, Jobs not only decreased the likelihood of a power struggle and confusion, but also publicly selected and expressed confidence in a new leader. Had a successor not been waiting in the wings, it is likely that Apple stock prices would have dipped as news of Jobs' death spread.

Life is unpredictable, and even young leaders and pastors in perfect health and with every intention of putting in several decades of service to the ministry, need to plan for unforeseen events. If you want to leave behind a healthy generational ministry that literally and figuratively outlives you, then it's important to start designing now.

Planning provides the luxury of being systematic when charting the course for the future, so that the indicated successor and future leader can be identified and prepared to lead the ministry to the next level.

This works for any size business, group, congregation, or ministry at any time. Don't get behind in this area. Life may just surprise you.

OUR MEA CULPA

When we meet with other pastors of churches and leaders of organizations, and the subject turns to transition, we are often asked about our individual transition stories. We have included a brief summation of those stories in the next Appendix, and we hope you gain a bit of insight by reading them, and how we each approached one of the most delicate and sensitive processes we have ever encountered as pastor/leaders ourselves. Those insights collectively serve as the basis of this book.

Most insightful and proactive leaders also ask us, "What would you do differently in your transitions if you were to do them over?" or, "What mistakes did you make?"

Well, looking back, there are some things each of us would have done differently given our unique circumstances, and we are sure we each made quite a few errors, unique to our situation, church, and transition process. We certainly don't want the readers of this book to think we did everything right. However, what's embarrassing for each of us is the one common error we each made, and to our chagrin, we didn't even recognize we had made the mistake until well after we had each transitioned.

Sadly, while each of us took great care to ensure our own personal transition from the senior pastor role, as well as our successors transition to the new role of senior pastor, along with the elders and other leaders of the church to a successful transition conclusion—*we totally missed a crucial element*. The responsibility of helping our spouses process the effect our transition would have on them, and their emotional health and well-being as they had to process their own transition process going forward.

Now don't misunderstand. Each of us certainly took a large amount of time talking to our spouses about our eventual transition. The timing, the mechanics of the process, the ramifications and goals we hoped to see accomplished in transition—all these things we discussed at length with our spouse prior to even initializing the transitions we were about to embark on. We each came into total agreement as couples that transition was right and timely and God-ordained, prior to initializing it. And in each of our cases, we (the authors) spent a considerable amount of personal time thinking through what post-church leadership roles would look like, what new avenues we'd like to pursue, and what the future held for us following a long tenure of church pastoring. In other words, we each prepared ourselves emotionally, financially, career-wise, and in a host of other ways so that our transition, emotionally, would be smooth and with minimal uncertainty, confusion and instability.

The problem was, we failed to address the same topics with our spouses in a much more complete way, and that oversight led to a short season of confusion, uncertainty, and unrest for our spouses.

Our spouses are given a variety of titles: Pastor's spouse, First Lady (Gentleman), Associate Pastor, Co-Pastor and so many more. No matter what level of previous involvement your spouse had while you served as the senior leader/pastor, no matter the title or non-title, it is a matter of undeniable fact that just by being your spouse, there existed in the mind of many other leaders and congregation members an assigned level of influence and opinion not afforded to other spouses. Her or his opinion are often consulted if for nothing more than to gain insight on how the senior leader/pastor was thinking on any given subject. And that opinion or influence, no matter if it is formally established or tacitly assumed, is as hard to transition away from as it is for you, the senior leader, to do.

For most senior leaders/pastors the responsibility they carry for a church is not seen by them as a job, but a calling. They genuinely feel 'called' to that church or that city. Additionally, their spouse will understand and relate to this same calling—because they do go as one, even though each partner exhibits different gifting, talents and interests, and more importantly, they do serve as one. More importantly, the spouse has often squashed or limited her/his opportunities and dreams in order to make the spouse/leader successful as pastor.

This is not to say that the spouse of the senior leader/pastor **must** transition when their spouse does. In our case, two of the spouses transitioned out of responsibility, oversight, and leadership at the same time as their spouse. One did not, and she continues to serve graciously and with wisdom in a capacity in the church her husband served, ministering effectively to this day in an area she felt strongly called to. She has astutely limited her ability to exhibit overall influence and has tactfully and publicly deferred to the new senior pastor and his spouse.

But maintaining some responsibility or ministry, or being done with all ministry and responsibility is one thing, while processing the significant life change that transition in ministry represents is something totally different. It will require a strong and deliberate checkup of the emotional intelligence of the spouse, just as it was critical to do the same with the senior leader. The feelings of disconnect and fear of what the future might hold are as real with the spouse of the senior leader as they are with that senior leader. And just having a conversation with your spouse about your intentions for transition as a senior leader will not cut it if you hope to walk hand-in-hand into your future with your spouse. In other words, your transition is not just about you, senior leader, it's not just about your team or your congregation but first and foremost it is also about your spouse and the post-life she/he and you will both enjoy together.

Questions that must be asked and addressed include:

- What will we both do post-transition?
- What ministry outlet will we each require?
- What are the dreams we still each which to fulfill?

- How will we encourage and support each other in those dreams and their fulfillment?
- How will we relate to our friends and fellow team members of the church we are transitioning from?
- What fears, concerns, thoughts, ideas, and struggles are we each facing?
- What do we want our lives and our marriage to look like 5, 10, 20 years from now?

Many of us have experienced the empty-nest syndrome in our own homes when the children we raised have grown up and are now their own person. They strike out on their own, leaving us alone again. For twenty years or so, we poured everything of ourselves into them, and they represented a great deal of our time, energy, and focus in life. The same is true of the church we have pastored. And when transition takes place, the sense of loss, uncertainty and unpredictability becomes pronounced. The fear of disconnection, of no longer being wanted or needed, and loss of a familiar identity is a part of the emotional health and wellness we must examine for ourselves, *and help our spouse examine it as well!*

If not, you may very well enjoy a successful transition as far as the church is concerned, but you may experience a total failure in your relationship with your spouse. The chances of having a successful transition as a team of husband and wife is diminished considerably when you don't consider your spouse through the full scope of leadership transition. Don't break your chain at home.

THE AUTHORS' PERSONAL TRANSITION STORIES

MY STORY: STEPHEN M. STELLS, DMIN

The excitement and joy of seeing lives transformed through sharing the gospel was addictive. The work of discipleship, team building, leadership training, strategic planning for growth and interfacing with the community in a kingdom way—these caused the blood to pump through our veins. This precluded any notion of a day in the future when a thought about succession/transition would invade our space and change our rhythm of life. However, it happened to us, and it will happen to you.

To us, it was a devastating thought, and at the same time offered possibilities of a freedom we had not been afforded for thirty-five years. Pastors don't have weekends off. When growing up, our four children, often wondered aloud why everyone else went to the beach on sunny weekends except us. We did take appropriate vacation time yearly with them, however, outside of that, we were in church every weekend.

My first thought about succession occurred when I was twenty-seven years old and two years into pastoring our church. A gentleman who was a Prudential Insurance representative walked into my office and said, "My son and daughter-in-law attend your church, and I thought I would stop in to inquire about your retirement plan." I had not thought about retirement and had no plan for it. That day he set up an IRA for me that I couldn't touch until age 65. I contributed to it each month and still do, to this day. At the time, I thought I was wasting good money that I needed to support my family, but I kept at it. Looking back today, that man is one of my heroes.

The next time a thought of succession re-entered my thinking was when my oldest son was in his last semester at the University of Richmond, During that term, graduating seniors are sought after by the business community regionally. The university works hard to ensure that their graduates are well placed. One of the many things that they offer their graduating students is a final semester Job Fair, where regional corporations who are looking to hire, attend and interview students. Introductions are made and interviews ensue.

We were excited that our son, who had a high grade-point average in the Jepson School of Business Leadership was being afforded such an opportunity. He communicated how his friends were getting unbelievable job offers but was saying nothing about his own. Towards the end of the Job Fair, we were very concerned and asked if he had offers he was entertaining. To our surprise and shock, he said, "I'm not looking for a job in the business world, I've always wanted to be a pastor and I want to work on your church staff."

This announcement sent "shock and awe" through us. It left our emotions running the gamut. However, succession/transition instantly became a permanent part in our scope of thinking and strategic planning. I went to our board and told the story and asked for their advice. The church hired my son.

He was under the authority of the executive pastor and was assigned the work that no one else on staff wanted to do. I vacillated back and forth about his decision for ministry. Once or twice I thought about asking the executive pastor to put my son in a position to make him reconsider, so he would go out and get a job with great pay and benefits. Instead, over the next twelve years, my son worked in virtually every department of the church and excelled. His training in leadership at the University of Richmond had prepared him well.

As his tenure working for the church increased, so did his credibility with the board, the staff and the congregation. Over time, we realized that his viewpoint and approach to ministry was of great value to us and others. He wasn't trying to be THE leader, but he was becoming a very good leader. Skepticism in the beginning had turned to genuine respect, and respect was turning into trust. Trust in the kingdom is the commodity of exchange. It is virtually impossible to lead without the trust of those you are attempting to lead. While getting practical training working at the church, my son was also doing a Master of Theology degree through a modular program at Oral Roberts University. In his ninth year of working at the church, we felt it was time to start the succession /transition process.

Our decision to proceed with the succession/transition plan was one of the most emotionally difficult decisions Sharon and I ever made. Was the timing of all of this right? Was our son's maturation in ministry sufficient to carry the church forward in the time frame we were projecting? Did we have a plan to guide the process? How were we to go about creating the proper atmosphere that would unify the leaders, department heads, staff, and congregation?

We hoped to complete the succession/transition plan honorably above all else. We wanted to start and complete the process in an emotionally healthy way for ourselves, our leaders and the congregation. We worked hard to create channels for clear, continual and caring communication to the appropriate people at the appropriate time. The core values of the church mattered to us, as well as clear vision. Careful financial planning and a way to manage and measure progress on the succession journey was prioritized. It was important to design the succession/ transition in as orderly a way as possible.

To accomplish that goal, our church history, present and future, was vital. We wanted our congregation and community to view the succession/transition journey as a continuum, rather than a fragmented reconstruction of values, vision, mission and directional changes made by the successor. We determined to do everything possible to reflect transparency, honesty, integrity and honor in the succession/transition journey. We wanted our church to maintain a strong chain of influence in the community, and knew it started with how we handled our leadership.

To help us construct the succession/transition design, an outside consultant was brought in. We initiated the plan by agreeing to allow the consultant to interview thirty to fifty couples or singles across the generational spectrum, about their views of the church. They were encouraged to define it in their own words.

When the interview results were compiled and reviewed we recognized the need to redefine and clarify our values, vision, mission and philosophy of ministry. Some described the church as a mission's church, others as a hospital for the broken, while still others as a word church, and on and on it went. We needed to realign our people and the ministries of the church to our vision, mission and purpose. This required us to revisit our core values and determine what was negotiable and what was non-negotiable.

When this was done, we reflected on our history, where we were at present, and connected our past and present to the vision for the future (20 years out) as a continuum. We allowed for methodological adaptations without violating scripture, doctrine, or doing violence to our history. The importance of this was that the successor would have a roadmap forward that would be flexible enough to allow room to adapt to societal and cultural shifts, retaining relevance, while remaining grounded to the history and sacrifice of those upon whose shoulders he/she is standing. In doing so, the efforts of the predecessors are honored. When the comprehensive plan was completed, the board, staff and pastors began to gradually align people and ministries to the new vision plan without announcing the transition.

The plan called for a three-year transition period. The first-year strategy was simply to have my son preach three times in the Sunday services in the first six months and six times in the last six months. The second year he would preach one Sunday each month and visit our mission churches in India, Africa, and Europe to be abreast of the ongoing mission efforts of our church. The third year he was to preach twice each month and begin to head up the elders' meetings and have access to all ministry meetings associated with our church. The last six months he was to lead all meetings on finance appropriation and all church ministry matters. All of this was probationary, meaning that, if for some reason, he was to drive the bus in the ditch, we could intervene and reset the transition date.

Different levels of leadership were presented with the plan, asked for input, support and prayers, and informed of the actual transition at different times. Leaders were communicated with as we went down the leadership and volunteer structure. After all the leaders were presented with the plan, we approached the non-leadership influencers in the church, and presented our plan to them. When each level of leadership and the influencers were on board with the succession/transition plan, we announced an all church meeting six months before the transition service. We shared, the process, the levels of leadership we had worked through, ending with the complete succession/transition plan. We assured them that the church was poised for a very bright future and asked them for their support and prayers. We informed them that their questions, concerns and suggestions were welcome, and they could talk to anyone in leadership with whom they felt comfortable.

Our people were amazingly appreciative of the three-year body of work we produced and our attention to detail with their wellbeing in mind. They appreciated the sensitivity to the church's history and the re-clarification of vision and mission and that there would be no sudden knee-jerk directional or philosophical changes.

We completed the succession/transition plan with a Saturday night service in honor of the thirty-eight years Sharon and I served as the lead pastors. It was an amazing service attended by all of our church plant pastors, as well as our congregation. We were honored and prayed over for the next chapter in our lives. When we left the service that night, a weight that we hadn't really realized we had carried was lifted. We sensed the favor of the Lord and a calm assurance that we had successfully passed the baton to the next generation.

The next day (Sunday) attention shifted to the setting in service for our son and daughter-in-law. The atmosphere was electric as people poured in to witness this generational exchange in the lead role of the church. A pastor well-known by our church, preached that day. He affirmed the new pastors and the congregation and its vision going forward. Prayer over my son and daughter-in-law by the eldership and visiting pastors was off the charts. Tears of joy flowed down nearly every face there. We left with a feeling of assurance concerning the future of the church and God's favor on us all.

On Monday, our feelings were different. Sharon and I, while happy with the results of the succession/transition plan, felt as if we had somehow lost our best friend. *What are we going to do now?* We wondered.

We were staying at the church and our role had been defined. We weren't the pastors and we weren't staff. However, we were the founders. and the elders' board and our new pastors wanted us to continue to attend and be in support of the leadership. We were asked to encourage people who came to the church during our watch, giving my son time to establish a true trust relationship with them as their pastor. We have become the best cheerleaders for the entire leadership team.

There has been continual growth, including another campus that is doing very well, and a plan to start four more in our area. We also lead the church's missions network team and are enjoying helping to extend its mission reach.

The succession/transition plan and the execution of it was amazing, but unfortunately, there were a few people that saw the transition as a place to make a change and did so. We were disappointed, but in our heart of hearts knew that God's favor was with us. The effect of the few who did leave was barely noticeable and the excitement and momentum actually increased.

Our church has more than doubled as of this writing. A new campus is growing exponentially, and His grace and faithfulness continues to abide with us.

What brings me great joy is my work through Seira Group LLC, and a partnership with two of the most incredible former lead pastors of great churches, Dr. Jerry David and Pastor Mike Servello. We have taken our collective experiences and the wisdom gleaned from them and are making a difference consulting churches across the country which are considering succession/transition. To see the generational leadership baton passed correctly, without loss of momentum, in a transparent, honest, orderly and honorable way, defines the thrill of victory for all of us.

The "what's next" question is answered for us, and this fairly new chapter is even more exciting than the last one. However, we also know that the last chapter was essential to setting up this one. The chapters of this book were not borrowed from someone else's experience. We all actually lived it, loved it, learned from it, and now give it to you for consideration.

MY STORY: JERRY W DAVID, DMIN

We successfully transitioned the leadership of our church in January 2014, after twenty-five years of pastoring in Lincoln, Nebraska. My wife and I founded the church in 1989 and we were certainly surprised by how fast those years flew by as we stood proudly that January day, and laid hands on the new leaders and their team.

I knew early on as we planted, that we were to build a generational church, one not centered around a personality but around the name of Jesus Christ. I realized that that commitment would one day involve being deliberate and strategic when looking to step down and transition to that next generation. So almost from the beginning of our tenure, I knew in the back of my mind that I was going to have to seek a way to make the eventual transition successful.

Approximately five years from when I wanted to step down and when it would be appropriate to do so, I began to list the values that would be important to me. I needed to ensure they were visible and identifiable in the church and its leadership prior to transition, and to make sure those same standards were "valuable" and non-negotiable to the next generation. Since I had a good, general idea of who would be a part of the next generation leadership, I began to meet with them and talk to them in-depth about each and every principle. I made it clear to them why those values existed, what they meant to us, and why even though the implementation of those values might be different one day, the values themselves should not change.

To me, this is the real reason transitions are often not successful. There is a lack of understanding and fidelity to the values that church or organization has been built on. It is what attracted people and families to participate and would prompt them to continue to do so. Too often though, a new leadership team (typically a young and inexperienced team) comes and looks to make their mark as new leaders. And rather than just putting forth a new vision or a new emphasis to spur growth or influence in the community they begin to dismantle values. This is a train-wreck waiting to happen.

Values become the stabilizing force in any organization that keeps people committed, loyal and productive. People are usually willing and open to try new approaches and ideas, particularly when a new team is placed into leadership. But start messing with the values, and the work will implode.

In my case, after several years of meeting with the new and younger team members, it became clear who the leader of that team should be. However, to test my thinking and see if I was clearly hearing from God about the matter, I asked two leaders in that group to pray, asking if they should be the next senior pastor and get back to me with their answer.

Thankfully, one came back and said, "it's not me," and the other said "it's me." I'm not sure what I would have done if both had said yes or no, but I didn't have to cross that bridge. The one who said yes was the one I knew the Lord had indicated to me as the one to lead.

Once this was established, I began to include him and his wife in a much more deliberate way. Our communication became more intense and more consistent. His responsibility with the pulpit and guest ministers began to change, and I gave him more and more input. In fact, the last year of us leading side-by-side, I had him set the preaching/teaching calendar for the year and I submitted to it. It was fun to watch him process these new areas of responsibility. He felt good about doing so, knowing I was still around as a safety net for him.

The elders and ministry team gelled around him and his wife nicely during this time. In fact, at our last elders' retreat, about four months from my eventual stepping aside, the elders collectively suggested that

I make this my last official eldership meeting, allowing the new leader to begin running all future assemblies as well as setting the agenda.

At first, I must admit I was a bit taken back. But in thinking it thorough I knew what they were telling me was that I had done a good job preparing the new leader and they now trusted him as they did me. In other words, it was a compliment to me to be asked to step aside.

Quickly after, a date was set on the calendar for our transition service. Events were planned, guests were invited, and the church was informed of all that would soon be taking place. Because the new leader had already taken on so much private and public responsibility, the announcement was not a shock. The opposite was true—the church responded with joy and a standing ovation when the announcement was made, and we never looked back!

A significant part of our story comes from the fact that our church at the time of the transition enjoyed a demographic of about 52% African-American congregants. Growing up in Detroit, I had lots of interface with the African-American church community, and I was well aware that once you are their pastor, they are hard-pressed to accept anyone else. I love them for this, but I knew change was necessary.

As it happened, the new leader I was about to install was African (Kenyan) while I was white, but that wasn't about to make him a "shoe-in", especially with my older African-American congregants. Knowing this, about eight months prior to our transition, I decided to invite all our members 55 years and older, to an event just for them at the church. We announced a dinner with the pastor night and made sure as many of our congregants as possible in this age group (white and black), would be able to attend.

When they arrived, they were greeted with beautifully decorated tables and gifts at each place setting. They were fed a delicious catered meal, served by our youth who were dressed as servers and did an outstanding job. Following the meal, my wife and I announced that we felt the Lord indicated to us our time as pastors was soon going to be over and we would be turning the responsibility over to the newer and next generation.

I made no mention of "who" that would be (although they asked), but what I did ask them to do with me, was work hard at making the 'next generation' successful. This included stopping any gossip they heard when they heard it, speaking only positive things to their friends and fellow congregants about the new leadership, and being a verbal and present encourager to the new younger leaders every chance they got.

When I imparted this vision to them, setting the scene of us working together on it, I all but insured a successful transition and reduced the loss of any members who wouldn't be on board. In other words, together, we determined to create an atmosphere of honor and order concerning the new leaders. This caused a chain reaction, where the younger generation honored myself and those in my age group even more so.

To this day, almost five years later, the church is growing, the old and young are still worshipping together, and the demographics remain the same (multi-ethnic). The new senior leader and his team are well respected, received, and esteemed. As a founder of such a great church—I couldn't be prouder!

MY STORY: MIKE SERVELLO

We started pastoring our church in November of 1980, beginning with a group of twenty people, in an abandoned four-story school building that was "gifted" to us. Slowly, we grew from 20 to 75 over a five-year period. Then we built our new church—which became the first new one built in our community in over fifty years. Soon after our church grew to about 400.

As our church grew, we merged our ministry with two other long-time pastor friends, bringing three congregations together into one location. During this season, we decided to build another new church in Utica, N.Y.

In the ten years following, we steadily grew, building with the strategy of touching our city and region. We wanted to raise up a generational church that would be here long after the original team passed off the scene.

Beginning in 2003, we began to have discussions as a leadership team, thinking about the future—dropping seeds in minds that we needed to be planning long-term for the future of the church. It was evident to our team that the next leader should be my son, this was confirmed again and again, both by the obvious grace on his life to lead and feed the congregation, but prophetically as well.

Our church had grown gradually and steadily over the decades, from one campus to five in four different cities, with multiple staff and a global outreach. Because of the size and scope of our ministry, we understood the next leader would need to rise through the ranks slowly and carefully.

Over the next years, I began carefully delegating authority and responsibility for the various areas of leadership to my son in stages: leading the staff, preaching regularly, deciding sermon series, choosing guest ministries, determining aspects of annual budgets, vision casting, and then choosing his own leadership team. This allowed him to digest each aspect of what he was leading and then move on to the next. The process allowed him to grow into his new role, ready to guide our congregation into the future. Our transition took place in 2014, thirty years after I began. Often, we don't consider that what was built over decades can't be transferred quickly, if we want continuity and longevity.

The results of our transition are a testament to the goodness and faithfulness of God. By the time we actually conducted the formal transition, the majority of our people thought it had already happened. We had no significant loss of people, finances or momentum. In fact, the opposite is true. The church has grown significantly, and today, the attendance numbers are over multi-hundreds at almost every one of our campuses.

Post-transition, my wife and I enjoy a continued place of honor in the church we founded and help out when asked. We are also enjoying our role as grandparents more. Our son and his team are doing well. He's kept the original people and has added many more leaders that weren't in the church during my time of leadership. The church continues to this day, now as a multi-site, multi-generational church with influence throughout the upstate New York region from Albany to Syracuse. Without an honorable design of succession planning, supported through the art and order of generational transition, none of the work continuing today would be possible.